A must-read – Simi's evidence-bas~~ ~ ~~ ~~ ~~ ~~ rm busy professionals, helping you achieve more of what matters, with more joy!

**Shadé Zahrai, co-founder of Influenceo Global and Peak Performance Educator for Fortune 500s**

Simi touches the human soul and heart without any judgement. Her 5Q approach is simple and practical and helps you design your day for impact and joy.

**Elif Kaypak, VP Global Marketing, Coca-Cola Brand**

An easy to follow, well written, helpful and practical guide for self-awareness and improvement. In 5 minutes each morning Simi's 5Qs Formula has the potential to change your life, bringing you more joy and fulfilment in all aspects of your life.

**Aylin Bagdadi, General Manager Community Development & Partnerships, Western United FC**

A fantastic tool for any busy professional looking to optimise their experience of, and output from, their working life. I have found the simple and pragmatic framework invaluable in helping me to continue to become the professional, leader, and person I aspire to be.

**Chris Jewel-Clark, Legal and General PLC**

*Productivity Joy* will inspire and empower you to unlock your full potential. Simi's 5Qs Formula is a game-changer. I wholeheartedly recommend *Productivity Joy* to anyone looking to transform their mindset and embrace a more productive, joyful existence.

**Emma McQueen, Business Coach**

In the midst of a staggering rise in burnout globally, Simi Rayat has written a compelling guide with *Productivity Joy*. While most begin their day by reaching for their phone, inundated with negative news, the 5Qs Formula offers a crucial hack. It is an effective, important, and highly enjoyable book.

**Sophie Krantz, Global Strategist**

Simi Rayat's 5Qs formula has been a game-changer for me, helping me create a clear path to my goals and unlock my strengths. With its practical and inspiring approach, this book has become my go-to guide for daily motivation and focus.

**Teg Sethi, General Manager, Endoca AU**

Joy and Productivity! Two core elements to doing work we love. When everything we do becomes a labour of love, it doesn't feel like work.

**Matt Church, founder, Thought Leaders**

In a world where leaders are stressed, overworked, and struggling, this book offers a clear pathway to becoming a more present, resilient, and empathetic leader. After using the 5Qs Formula for just the past two weeks, I can testify that the clarity of purpose it provided was unlike anything I have experienced!

**Ajit Dodani, Empathy Strategist©,
founder and CEO, EmpathifyU**

In today's busy world, finding balance is extremely important, but becoming exceedingly difficult. Simi's 5Qs approach provides an easy but deliberate way to find this balance and set the foundations for success each day.

**Abhineet Singh Lekhi,
Senior Business Leader**

# Productivity
# JOY

# Productivity

# JOY

Feel Energised
and Be Effective in
5 Minutes a Day

## Simi Rayat

PSYCHOLOGIST

WILEY

A catalogue record for this book is available from the National Library of Australia

*Registered Office*
John Wiley & Sons Australia, Ltd. Level 4, 600 Bourke Street, Melbourne, VIC 3000, Australia

For details of our global editorial offices, customer services, and more information about Wiley products visit us at www.wiley.com.

Wiley also publishes its books in a variety of electronic formats and by print-on-demand. Some content that appears in standard print versions of this book may not be available in other formats.

Cover design by Wiley
Cover image (glitter): © Thanakorn/Adobe Stock
Cover and internal image (sun rays): © moonnoon/Adobe Stock

Set in Plantin Std 10.5/16pt by Straive
Printed and bound by CPI Group (UK) Ltd, Croydon, CR0 4YY

C9781394282210_021024

*When you make people feel they matter, we all achieve extraordinary things.*

*I'm sincerely grateful to all those who have made me feel that I matter, and have made me feel seen, heard and valued.*

# Contents

| | |
|---|---|
| *Acknowledgements* | *xi* |
| *About the author* | *xiii* |
| *Preface* | *xv* |
| *Introduction* | *xix* |

## **Part I: Setting the foundations**     **1**

| | | |
|---|---|---|
| 1 | Getting to know the 5Qs Formula | 3 |
| 2 | Using the questions and this book effectively | 15 |

## **Part II: The 5Qs Formula**     **21**

| | | |
|---|---|---|
| 3 | Checking your emotional temperature | 23 |
| 4 | Gratitude shapes your brain | 57 |
| 5 | Cultivating positivity and personal growth | 83 |
| 6 | Increasing productivity and joy | 119 |
| 7 | Setting your compass | 159 |

# Part III: Additional aspects to consider   191

8   Your oxygen mask    193

9   End the day on reflection    209

*Conclusion*    *217*

*Appendix: Typical values*    *221*

*Further reading*    *225*

*5Qs template*    *227*

*Work with Simi*    *231*

*Index*    *233*

# Acknowledgements

To my beloved husband, Harvin. You have been my harshest critic yet biggest supporter, always challenging me to grow. You are not just my rock but also my strength and inspiration. Thank you for all your love, support and humorous antics.

To my cherished sons, you both are my greatest teachers. While I strive to guide you towards greatness, you unknowingly guide me towards becoming the best version of myself. You both make me hugely proud, and I can't wait to see you both use your superpowers to positively impact this world.

To my parents, I am eternally grateful for your love and encouragement, even across the oceans. My mother's strength and my father's wisdom have acted as two wings of a butterfly, supporting me to fly high and live my dreams. To my brother, your commitment to your values continues to inspire me, and so does my nephew's love.

To my family in Australia, I look forward to watching all the kids grow and creating beautiful memories. A special thank you to my sister-in-law for your friendship and kindness.

I deeply thank all my extended family and friends for their continual support throughout my journey. Your presence in our lives, near and far, has been a source of strength and encouragement.

My special appreciation goes to all my clients for entrusting me, having the courage to be vulnerable, and being committed to their transformation.

I am deeply grateful to beautiful souls such as Vino, Harlin Auntie and Amrit Uncle, whose unconditional love, support and friendship have enriched my life beyond measure.

A big thank you to all my mentors, teachers and leaders who have believed in, guided and championed me. A special mention to one of my earlier managers, Alyson Wells—you truly made me feel seen, heard and valued at the onset of my career as an organisational psychologist.

A huge thank you to *you* for picking up this book.

Stay in touch at www.simirayat.com.

# About the author

Simi Rayat is a chartered organisational psychologist renowned as a leading executive leadership coach and keynote speaker based in Australia. With over two decades of expertise in leadership development, coaching, entrepreneurship and fostering inclusive cultures, Simi is the founder of SimiRayat.com, a thriving psychology consulting and coaching practice. Passionate (some would argue obsessed) and dedicated, Simi transforms leaders into ones who are a joy to work for and do business with, helping them to develop their emotional intelligence to drive better results, relationships and revenue. As a result, these leaders inspire people to give their best and achieve extraordinary feats because they feel seen, heard and valued in their presence.

Having worked and lived across the United Kingdom, Canada and Australia, Simi serves a global clientele of leaders including those who work for Fortune 500 companies, multinational financial and professional services firms and public sector organisations, alongside accelerating scale-ups in Australia. Her profound ability to forge deep connections, empathise and guide individuals and teams towards transformation sets her apart. Simi's authentic approach fosters an environment where even the most seasoned or less self-aware clients feel comfortable and safe in dropping their guard, opening up and experiencing unparalleled transformation.

Beyond her professional pursuits, Simi finds fulfilment in her roles as a devoted wife and mother to two young boys. She loves to share many moments of laughter, enjoys being close to the water, indulging in wholesome cuisine and nurturing meaningful relationships with family and friends.

# **Preface**

*Are you surviving or thriving? Are you truly living life, personally and professionally, or are you constantly greasing the wheels, feeling like you are rushing from one thing to the next?*

I vividly remember waking up one cold Saturday morning in autumn in our two-bedroom flat in Chiswick, London. As I approached the window and pulled back the blind, a thin film of water obscured my view of the usually bustling high street below. Wiping away a patch of condensation with my hand, I couldn't shake the feeling of tightness in my throat—a familiar sensation of fear creeping in.

I knew what I feared, yet I hesitated to confront it. The answer to this question is what I truly feared: was I genuinely living, or was I merely surviving?

Despite the outward appearance of success—a thriving business, a supportive husband and two wonderful children—I felt an almost constant sense of unrest within me. My inner turmoil had begun to seep into various aspects of my life, even earning me the nickname 'the bull' from my immediate family. While they would tease me with this name as I'd enter the room, it was a painful reminder for me of my reactive nature and this dark shadow of energy I was carrying during this phase of my life, in my mid-30s. Even though I was a practising psychologist, I was neglecting my own wellbeing. I was failing to practise what I preached to others.

Somewhere along the way, in the midst of major life transitions (migrating countries three times, getting married, growing and selling my first business, becoming a mother...), I had lost myself. Born in the early 1980s in Leeds, Yorkshire, in the United Kingdom, I enjoyed a childhood filled with love and care from both my immediate and extended family. At five years old, my family and I moved to a small village on the outskirts of Leeds, where my father had secured a teaching role. Most of the village had heard of us, 'the Indian family', before we had even got to know or meet them. I was the only Indian girl in my primary and later high school. No-one else looked like me.

Shortly after moving in, we learned that a few villagers had started a petition against us moving there due to our ethnicity. Thankfully, not many people signed the petition. Though my parents shielded my brother and me from most discussions, I clearly recall an overwhelming desire to belong and be accepted in our new community. I wanted to matter, and to feel valued and recognised.

Despite the initial adversity, my family quickly integrated into the neighbourhood, and I look back on my upbringing with overall happiness and positivity. From an early age, I discovered joy in reading books. Looking back, and after exploring psychological research on empathy development and its connection to reading fiction, I realised that this is where my strength of empathy began to form, and also my interest in what others were thinking and feeling.

At age 16, I became fascinated by the field of personal and professional development when I discovered Stephen Covey's *The 7 Habits of Highly Effective People*. Inspired by the transformative insights of this book, I became determined to pursue my passion for personal development, which was quite different from what I was learning at school. I convinced my parents to let me leave school to start my first job—as a customer service assistant at Halifax Bank. Interacting with customers, especially the elderly, taught me the actual value of empathy, meaningful interactions and strong leadership.

Sparked by these learnings, I returned to education, to study business management and psychology. Guided by inspiring teachers, I pursued internships and a degree in organisational psychology and management at the University of Leeds. I secured an internship with a Canadian leadership consultancy and saw the reality of building a career in my area of passion. I knew firmly that I wanted to pursue a career where I could grow myself, in order to help others to grow. I then completed a master's in organisational psychology at Nottingham University.

A pivotal moment arose when I met my now-husband Harvin. Together, we made the life-altering decision to migrate to Australia, leaving behind everything and everyone I knew in the United Kingdom. While I seemed to adapt outwardly to this move, internally I grappled with profound loneliness and a sense of disconnection, longing for the familiar comforts of home. Nonetheless, I secured a role with a leading management consulting firm and, over time, forged meaningful friendships and relationships, gradually feeling more settled in Australia.

The birth of my son, however, ignited a longing for a deeper sense of belonging, prompting mine and Harvin's decision to return to live in the United Kingdom. In the middle of all these life changes, we experienced a few challenges in our marriage and sought couples counselling. As a psychologist, I was accustomed to delving into the lives of others, offering empathy and support, yet sharing my own personal experiences felt unfamiliar and unsettling, and it took me a while to lean into the spirit of the counselling support. Being vulnerable and open to receiving support was not something I had done before, and I knew I needed to work on this.

Being back in London, and now with our second child, grounded our family, connected us, and allowed us to explore parts of Europe. However, my entrepreneurial drive remained steadfast. In 2018, I left my corporate role and founded my current business, SimiRayat.com. I worked with leaders and teams across the United Kingdom and Europe to enhance leadership impact, wellbeing and inclusion.

Through all of this outward success, and even when witnessing my clients' transformative growth brought immense satisfaction, I couldn't shake a sense of personal incompleteness and disappointment. I had hindered my own progress and fallen short of my fullest potential. I knew I had failed to achieve the level of progress I had expected for myself at the stage of life I was in. I had neglected to nurture and practise self-development, especially through the significant transitions I had experienced in my own life.

As I stood there at the window, facing my own internal battles, deep down, I knew I needed to change. I had to face the truth—I was merely surviving when all I truly desired was to thrive. I yearned to feel fully present and connected, to achieve all my goals, and to be the most impactful version of myself. My aspiration extended beyond fulfilling my own potential; I yearned to empower others to do the same, to live life to its fullest, because I knew, deep down, this could be truly possible. Yet, I understood the paradox: how could I truly help optimise others when I knew I hadn't fully optimised myself yet?

# Introduction

Do you feel like no matter how much you do, there is always so much more to do? Do you feel like it's only a matter of time before you drop one of the balls and forget something or let yourself or someone else down? Do you think you still have so much yet to accomplish but feel exhausted, drained and sometimes lack the motivation and energy to do what's in your heart? Do you wake up and not have time to even notice the roses, let alone smell them?

In this state, you're constantly in survival mode, completely caught up in the hustle and bustle of modern life. You constantly feel on edge, anticipating the next challenge or setback and struggling to find balance amid the chaos. Each day feels like a race just to get through to the end, not to stuff up, while barely keeping it all together. Yet somehow, along the way, you expect yourself to be calm, present, focused, productive and rational and do your best despite what life throws your way.

Being in a constant mode of survival is no fun; you are always on the lookout, on high alert, highly strung, and stuck in the reactive nature of the here and now. Constantly feeling like this takes a toll on your emotional, mental and physical health, which in turn affects your ability to do and achieve your best. Your productivity suffers, as does your wellbeing. Your relationships also suffer, as those closest to you often bear the brunt of your abrupt or reactive responses.

As I outline in the preface, I was intimately familiar with this state. I also knew my story was not mine alone, and it served as an important reminder that even those who appear to have it all together can battle internal struggles in silence. Finding solace in this realisation, I understood that acknowledging my own challenges was where I would find true strength and resilience. By taking proactive steps forward, even if they were small, I could begin to break free from stagnation and feel empowered and energised.

At this very moment, I realised I had the power to create something truly transformative, a tool that went beyond mere survival and could unlock the full potential of the human mind and spirit to help myself—and others—thrive. Having counselled and coached countless individuals through their own struggles, I knew I possessed a wealth of knowledge and insight that could benefit me in my current phase of life and serve as a beacon of hope for others. With each person I had helped over the years, I had gained invaluable insights into the intricacies of the human psyche, and now it was time to apply that wisdom to my own life. I knew that by using my journey and the lessons I learned along the way, I could find a way to inspire others to reap the benefits of transforming their mindsets for optimal daily living.

This realisation prompted me to question how our brains could be primed for greatness at the start of the day, when they are at their most malleable. Before being distracted by the challenges of the day, how could we activate and optimise our brain in a way that helps us to thrive? I started to explore the daily rituals of high-performing professionals. Through research into existing morning routines and beyond, I identified a gap: the absence of a reliable, science-backed method to prime the brain at the start of the day, to foster daily productivity and happiness.

I felt a genuine renewed sense of purpose and determination, and set out to develop an effective, simple and practical approach to a morning formula. It would not only nourish my mindset but also empower me to break free from the constant cycle of survival. This led to the development of my 5Qs Formula, and during this process I underwent my own transformation. After a long time, I finally experienced a profound sense of internal alignment, harmonising both my heart and head. I did the deep inner work to develop my impact, cultivate emotional connection, find balance, maintain rational thinking even during high pressure and stress, and embrace my inner strength. Importantly, once developed, I knew I could then pass on this formula to others.

As I worked through the process of developing and fine-tuning the formula, leaning heavily into psychology, neuroscience and my leadership experience, I knew that its principles were not just meant for me alone; they were meant to be shared with the world. Each insight gained from my years of counselling, mentoring and coaching hundreds of individuals became the building block, a cornerstone in the foundation of this transformative formula.

## Introducing the 5Qs Formula

The 5Qs Formula is a science-backed, proven formula to prime the brain, unlock the full potential within and cultivate an intentional and optimistic mindset to maximise daily productivity and happiness. The formula derives its name from its five core questions, each designed to catalyse self-reflection, priming, accountability and daily personal growth. The 5Qs Formula helps you do more of what matters, magnifies your joy and helps you be 5 per cent better each day.

You can think of the 5Qs Formula as a compass that guides you through the vast sea of daily life. By starting your day with taking stock of your emotional state (question one), acknowledging the winds of gratitude (question two), assessing your current position and trajectory (question three), plotting your course with specific goals (question four) and finally setting sail with intention and purpose (question five), you ensure that you're steering towards your desired direction for the day ahead. Without this intentional navigation at the outset of your day, you risk drifting aimlessly or being at the mercy of the external currents. By starting the day with the 5Qs Formula, you can gain a clear sense of direction, empowerment and resilience, enabling you to navigate life's challenges and opportunities with clarity and purpose.

The five questions in the formula are as follows:

- *Question 1:* What is your emotional temperature, and what are you feeling today?

- *Question 2, parts A and B:* What experiences, things or people in your life are you grateful for because they inspire you to be a better version of yourself? Think of a time you have received gratitude and appreciation from someone; how did it make you feel?

- *Question 3:* What is working well for you right now, and what could be working better for you?

- *Question 4:* What three things do you want to achieve today?

- *Question 5:* How will you show up today?

Through focusing on these questions, the 5Qs Formula provides a reliable, science-backed solution to prime your brain to address productivity issues, energy stagnation and interpersonal communication issues. And it only takes five minutes a day! Ultimately, these five minutes spent priming your brain can help you lead a more fulfilling and successful life.

And you can even use the following PRIME acronym as a memory prompt when you first start out:

- **P:** Pinpoint emotions and feelings.

- **R:** Recognise gratitude.

- **I:** Identify what is working and could be working better.

- **M:** Make a list of three high-impact tasks for today.

- **E:** Envision how you want to show up today.

After outlining some of the basics in part I of this book, each of the chapters in part II is dedicated to one of the 5Qs Formula questions, to help you understand why the question is important and how it helps you maximise your productivity and joy. I've also included lots of examples throughout the book, taken from my own experience and the many clients I've worked with. (All names have been changed.) These examples, along with the self-reflection exercises through the book, help you to get started and apply the learning to your own experience.

# Getting primed to act — from the start of your day

Have you been to a restaurant, looked at the menu, and been completely spoilt for choice on what to order, because everything sounds so delicious and appealing? Being a vegetarian for my entire life, I've often found myself at restaurants only being able to choose from one or two vegetarian meals on the menu, especially when growing up in the United Kingdom in the 1980s and 1990s. However, after migrating to Melbourne, Australia, in 2009 and settling into the northern suburbs, I found myself in a bohemian area with fully vegetarian restaurants, where I could actually order anything from the entire menu.

Because this was a rare situation to be in, I excitedly read and re-read the menu to see what dish I really wanted to order. I found myself in the unusual situation of having too many choices and, in a sense, I was stuck in the decision-paralysis mode by my overwhelming options. It took me so much longer to decide because I had too many other similarly attractive food options. I procrastinated in making a decision, and then second-guessed my decision, overthinking what I would really like. All this deliberation over a simple menu choice—clearly a 'first world issue' to contend with.

This sort of decision-paralysis—and sometimes over the smallest of choices—is far from unusual, however. In fact, research shows we make over 3500 decisions per day, most of which are not of high impact or relevance, or conducive to productivity, wellbeing and relationships. When faced with too many choices, and especially when the options are more similar than dissimilar, most people find making a decision that much harder. This concept is very important to understanding the effectiveness of the 5Qs Formula, because this formula requires you to choose and make a series of small yet highly impactful and intentional decisions at the start of your day. Making these decisions warms up your decision-making muscles, empowers and primes you, and provides you with a sense of control, autonomy and liberation—all from the very start of your day.

Each time you decide to apply the 5Qs Formula and answer each of the questions within it, you enable your brain to experience a neurochemical boost, a dopamine hit, which motivates you to make another decision and another decision, propelling you to move forward, in an intentional, conscious way for your day ahead. Starting your day in this way creates momentum, motivation and progression, which are essential to all those who want to live a purposeful, fulfilled, present and productive day. Making such decisions at the start of your day kicks off the domino effect of further decisions being made throughout your day, whether this be at work or in your personal life. With each decision made, your accountability and ownership for each decision grows, and you become more confident in your decision-making capacity and capability. The 5Qs Formula provides you with a tool to take personal responsibility for how you experience your day and how others experience you. In this way, you give yourself the opportunity to do more of what matters to you and brings you joy and, in turn, you become a joy to be around.

So are you ready to learn how to apply the 5Qs Formula? I'll be right there with you, supporting you every step of the way. I'm genuinely excited for you to experience the transformative benefits of the 5Qs Formula, just like I and countless others have. Let's start on this process towards greater productivity, energy and fulfilment in your life. Let's begin!

# PART I

# Setting the foundations

# CHAPTER 1

# Getting to know the 5Qs Formula

Throughout the tumultuous upheaval of the global pandemic in 2020 and 2021, I had the opportunity to put my 5Qs Formula to the test on myself and with my clients. During this extraordinary time, I worked closely with my clients, guiding them through the formula's principles to develop an optimistic mindset among the myriad struggles brought about by the pandemic, alongside the usual daily work and personal challenges.

When I witnessed the positive results and profound impact of the 5Qs Formula on the individuals I coached and on myself, such as heightened focus, increased productivity, and enhanced energy levels, effectiveness, optimism and overall happiness, it further reinforced the importance of sharing this transformative approach with others, like you, who also deserve and desire to live a productive, happy, fulfilled and balanced life.

At first, I struggled to believe that such a transformation could be achieved in just five minutes at the start of each day. However, after hearing the feedback and experiences of those who applied the 5Qs Formula, my scepticism quickly dissipated. Once they understood how to respond to the questions, my clients really did find themselves completing the entire formula in just five minutes each day.

# Productivity versus burnout

The term 'productivity' is often used in various contexts, typically emphasising achieving more with less, whether that's time or resources. However, true productivity is more than just efficiency. It encompasses effectiveness and impact, coupled with feelings of joy, energy and fulfilment. Essentially, productivity is achieving your goals in a meaningful way while prioritising personal wellbeing.

When my family and I returned to live in Australia in 2021 (in the middle of the pandemic), I recognised a concerning trend: burnout rates had soured since the pandemic. Shockingly, 81 per cent of the Australian workforce was silently battling stress and burnout, paralleled by 93 per cent of the UK adult population experiencing symptoms of burnout. Even more recently, according to the 2024 Global Talent Trends report published by Mercer, an HR consulting firm, more than eight out of 10 employees (approx. 82 per cent) are at risk of burnout this year. Furthermore, research conducted by Finder in early 2023 revealed that 83 per cent of Australians struggled with severe procrastination issues, leading to staggering losses of up to $60 billion a year in productivity for businesses.

Maintaining focus and attention has become an ongoing challenge in our distracted world. This book aims to provide you with a proven formula for daily clarity, focus and attention. It's a valuable resource for you if you are seeking to enhance your productivity, energy levels and overall fulfilment.

As the economic climate changes, many organisations undergo structural changes, downsizing and redundancies, resulting in the existing workforce having to accomplish more with fewer resources. Through my work with both organisations and individual professionals, I've observed how this necessity to do more with less often leads to heightened levels of overwhelm, increased stress and eventual burnout. The 5Qs Formula serves as a solution to these issues, guiding you to identify your most pressing and high-impact daily tasks rather than feeling the need to tackle everything, and so fostering a more sustainable approach. By challenging conventional notions of time allocation, the 5Qs Formula encourages intentional decision-making, helping you prioritise impactful tasks and activities to enhance overall effectiveness.

Feeling overly stressed and like your to-do list is never-ending can have significant flow-on effects. It can affect how you perceive yourself, your confidence levels and your interactions with others and, in turn, the culture you create around you. By learning how to regulate your emotions on a daily basis, you gain valuable skills and insights into how to show up in your interactions more effectively. This then enables you to contribute to fostering positive and meaningful cultures both at home and in the workplace. In doing so, you create spaces where you and others not only survive but also thrive, even through times of high pressure and uncertainty.

# Recognising your 'aha' moment and getting started

Do you believe in New Year's resolutions? Have you ever caught yourself waiting for a specific occasion—such as the start of a new year, month, or even just a Monday—before starting a new diet, workout regime, or learning a new skill? You may convince yourself that beginning something new at the start of a fresh beginning is the best approach. However, this is your mind playing a trick on you, allowing you to procrastinate and delay doing something that will require you to step into some level of discomfort. This discomfort could be due to a change in routine, denying yourself something, or exerting your time and energy into an activity that may be unpleasant.

It's easy to talk yourself out of doing something new or different or uncomfortable, even when you know it's probably good for you in the longer term. Staying in your comfort zone, which you are used to, often feels much easier and simpler. However, if you stay in this comfortable zone for too long, you will become complacent and not accomplish what you really want to achieve.

Let me give you an example to highlight what I mean. Wayne, a middle-aged banker, has been wanting to start a new exercise routine for better health. He knows committing to regular workouts will benefit him in the long run, but the thought of getting out of bed early or finding time in his busy schedule feels daunting, although he would rarely admit to that in public. Instead, he continues with his familiar routine of lounging on the couch after work, watching Netflix and snacking on the easiest-to-access and often unhealthiest types of foods. While staying in his comfort zone may feel easier in the short term, over time Wayne will notice a decline in his energy levels and will feel less motivated and satisfied with his health, body image and fitness levels. Without stepping out of this comfort zone and exercising, he will risk becoming complacent and not achieving his actual desire, which is to feel good when he wears his new suit to work and feel that he's got the energy to be more active outside of work.

I've noticed a typical pattern when coaching ambitious professionals and leaders: a genuine commitment to change often arrives when individuals experience an 'aha' moment. This moment occurs when they realise that staying in their comfort zone has become uncomfortably disruptive to their lives. For instance, this moment might come after a health scare, prompting you to overhaul your diet and exercise habits, or after being passed over for a well-deserved promotion, which leads you to seek opportunities elsewhere. These 'aha' moments of insight are crucial catalysts for personal growth and transformation.

Recognising an 'aha' moment is pivotal. It signifies an opportunity for a breakthrough—and this is extremely exciting, although it may feel scary. It's exciting because it's a chance for you to break free from feeling stuck and move past the fear associated with change. When these moments occur, neurons in the brain fire together, creating new connections and insights. Embracing these moments and stepping out of your comfort zone allows for the emergence of new experiences and feelings, paving the way for your continued growth, development and elevation.

Perhaps you're experiencing one or more of the following feelings:

- overworked

- burnt out

- lacking presence

- reacting to situations and people

- directionless and unintentional

- depleted of energy

- unfulfilled

- stuck in a rut

- procrastinating

- overthinking

- struggling with productivity

- overwhelmed.

Experiencing any of these feelings is a clear sign it's time for you to start implementing a daily practice of the 5Qs Formula. If you're feeling stagnant, complacent or bored, it is likely because you're too comfortable or frustrated with your current situation. To break free from this rut, you must embrace growth to improve your current situation by stepping out of your comfort zone and into the realm of discomfort.

Recognising these feelings is your cue to initiate change, pursue a not-so-distant future of growth, happiness, fulfilment and productivity that is within reach, and start practising the 5Qs Formula each day.

# Overhauling the morning routine

When developing the 5Qs Formula, I went on a quest to find out what professionals, leaders, managers and business owners usually do to set themselves up for success each day. I asked this question of the many corporate leaders, successful business owners and motivated professionals I coach and mentor, including leaders ranging from emerging level to senior level executives and board members. The most common responses I heard included:

- have my morning coffee

- meditate

- go to the gym

- do yoga

- create my to-do list

- go for a jog or morning walk

- listen to my favourite podcast

- visualise my day

- review what I'd completed from my list the day before and identify what was still outstanding

- ask my team what they needed help with that day

- read the news

- eat a healthy breakfast

- go through my emails.

Do any of the activities just listed resonate with you? Perhaps you already incorporate some of these practices into your daily routine, or maybe you find yourself longing to make time for self-care before diving into your workday. Whether you have an existing morning routine or wish to establish one, the 5Qs Formula can seamlessly complement your current practices or serve as a standalone morning routine to intentionally prime your mindset and behaviours.

Many of the activities these leaders were doing helped them to feel physically energised and 'pumped' through exercise, calm and centred through meditation or yoga, or planned and organised through diary management. While some of these activities released feel-good endorphins, and loosened and relaxed limbs and muscles, what was commonly absent from what these leaders were already doing was a focused strategy that primed their 'mindset', psychological and emotional wellbeing up for the day ahead.

The 5Qs Formula shared in this book is recommended as an addition to the relaxation and/or physical activities you already do at the start of your day; therefore, it's important to recognise and repeat what works for you and add the 5Qs Formula to your existing routine.

If you don't have a morning routine, the 5Qs Formula provides a strong foundation to ensure your psychological and emotional wellbeing is acknowledged and primed for your day ahead, and you can then add in physical exercise and/or relaxation techniques as required, too.

# Defining what 'success' means for you

When I asked leaders the question, 'What do you currently do each morning to set yourself up for success?', many also reflected on the word 'success', and questioned what daily 'success' meant or looked like in their world. For some leaders and managers, success was defined as simply getting through the day without anything major happening in their team, avoiding a client complaint, resolving a staff issue, securing a sale or new client, or nailing a client pitch. Some were very open to sharing that the phrase 'daily survival' came to mind, rather than the word 'success'. Many were still recovering from the stress, pressure and burnout experienced from leading their teams and organisations through the recent global pandemic. For those in their thirties and forties, juggling family commitments, demanding jobs and businesses, caring for ageing parents and looking after their health often meant they found themselves in survival mode.

In these cases, simply surviving the day was their focus. If you can relate to that, it's important to acknowledge that you are merely 'surviving' each day. For things to shift so you experience a strong sense of 'thriving', a transformation in what you are currently doing is required—and you can start to experience such a transformation when you put the 5Qs Formula in place.

For the purposes of this book, I define success as a feeling of intentional and planned accomplishment, a positive energy that elates you with joy or a feeling of meaningful satisfaction that you have completed or progressed what you had set out to do. In this way, daily success can be experienced when you consistently apply the 5Qs Formula. In addition to success being defined as a feeling, it's also a process, a mindset, a way of behaving, thinking and being, which will help you achieve your desired outcomes. In this sense, success is not an 'end point'. When applied from the lens of the 5Qs Formula, success is a process you can control and enjoy each day.

Knowing that success is a process you can control and enjoy each day is liberating. So many daily factors that can potentially influence your 'success' are outside of your control, such as the weather, interest rates, pandemics, crises and other people's reactions. However, when you start applying the 5Qs Formula, you start to re-direct your focus and energy to the things you can control and, in turn, you experience greater self-agency and autonomy. You prime and enable yourself to thrive.

What I started to notice and hear from many leaders, professionals and business owners was that they didn't have a particular reliable structure, system, routine or strategy that they felt consistently set them up for success—that is, to be focused and productive and still feel energised and satisfied through to the end of the day. What was missing was a fail-proof formula that anyone could implement to ensure their mindset was primed and optimised for success each day. This was why I started sharing the 5Qs Formula with my clients—and why I'm sharing it with you now.

These five minutes that you invest in yourself at the start of your day set up your mindset and emotions for the day. When your mind is focused and your emotions are acknowledged, you will feel balanced and calm, yet energised to achieve your goals.

The 5Qs Formula is very practical. It can be applied by anyone who is committed to starting their day well and wants to stay energised, productive and intentional throughout the day.

One important note here, however: while all the strategies and tips in this book can significantly improve your mood and wellbeing, they are not a replacement for seeking professional help if needed. For guidance with clinical depression, stress and anxiety, please seek the advice of your GP and other healthcare providers.

# Making the 5Qs Formula your daily habit

To make something a habit, James Clear, in his award-winning book *Atomic Habits*, outlines 'four laws' to forming a habit. Here is how you can apply his four laws to help make the 5Qs Formula a daily habit for you:

1. *Make it obvious:* Place your 5Qs Formula questions on a wall that you see every day, and in your journal or notepad in an easy-to-access and easy-to-see place the night before so you see it first thing in the morning, together with your writing pen. (You can also download the 5Qs Formula poster from my website, and put it up in a prime spot—just go to www .simirayat.com.)

2. *Make it attractive:* Integrate the 5Qs Formula into activities you already enjoy or find fulfilling. For example, you could complete the questions while sipping your morning coffee or tea, during a peaceful moment of reflection before getting

out of bed, on your commute to work or after you've done school drop-off.

3. *Make it easy:* Learn quickly how to respond to each question by reading all the chapters of this book.

4. *Make it satisfying:* The sequence in which each question has been designed and layered is intentional, and completing the 5Qs Formula will not only provide immediate benefits but also sustain a lift in your mood, energy and focus throughout your day.

Remember, doing something different for the first time can feel clunky, tricky and somewhat daunting. Use the PRIME memory prompt from the introduction as needed in the first few days. Repeating the 5Qs Formula for a week or so will help you become familiar with the process and start memorising the five questions, ensuring you complete it in five minutes.

James Clear has another piece of advice here: 'Every action you take is a vote for the type of person you wish to become'. By committing to applying the 5Qs Formula each morning, you are actively voting to be an emotionally balanced, grateful, intentional, high-impact and productive person. You can start developing your identity as someone who values your own time, seeks to maximise your daily impact and possesses heightened emotional intelligence, facilitating the development of strong, meaningful relationships with the people around you.

Consistently demonstrating each of the qualities will help you experience joy, satisfaction, fulfilment and energy each day.

# CHAPTER 2

# Using the questions and this book effectively

The questions within the 5Qs Formula can help you boost productivity and fulfilment, and your self-awareness. In the following chapters, I outline the science behind the formula and, most importantly, how to apply and incorporate the questions into your daily routine. I also highlight other highly effective tools and strategies to enhance your wellbeing and impact. And I've included stories and examples from real people's lived experiences—the everyday heroes of everyday life. In this way, you can relate, connect and find yourself in the pages that follow. It's the everyday person who can and will go on to have an extraordinary impact in this world, and I know that is you!

As you read this book, you have opportunities to pause, self-reflect, get to know yourself better and think about things differently. While I appreciate it's tempting to skip past the self-reflection exercises in this book, because you are likely keen to learn and apply the

5Qs Formula, taking a few moments to complete each intentionally curated exercise will reveal a new insight about yourself for yourself.

These insights will help you grow and elevate your daily impact. My clients often hear me share the following: 'If you do the same things in the same way, nothing will change'. The insights and reflections in this book can lead to your transformation, just as they have for the hundreds of clients I have worked with, and also for myself. Read this book with a curious mind and open heart and commit to your own growth. You will benefit from this, and everyone else around you will too.

I also encourage you to keep a journal or a notebook next to you as you read through the book. This way, you can capture your notes, reflect on responses, and track your progress and thoughts. Feel free to highlight the relevant sections of the book or add notes to the margins (or use these types of functions if reading the ebook). This book has been structured and designed so you can easily refer back to key elements, insights and tips on practical application. Use it as a tool as you learn the 5Qs Formula fully and reap its maximum benefits in all aspects of your life.

# Setting yourself up for success

To effectively utilise this book and the 5Qs Formula, follow the following steps.

## Step 1: Read the book fully

Start by reading the book from cover to cover. This will give you a comprehensive understanding of the 5Qs Formula and its components. Also become familiar with all included figures, such as the Ring of Emotions and feelings figure provided in chapter 3.

## Step 2: Engage in self-reflection

As mentioned, I've provided self-reflection exercises throughout the book. These are designed to help you understand yourself better and apply the concepts discussed. Take the time to pause and intentionally complete each exercise.

## Step 3: Use a journal

Applying the 5Qs formula involves asking yourself five key questions at the start of your day. I recommend physically writing down your response to each question so you are actively engaged in processing your responses by getting them out of your head and onto paper or your preferred device. By actively recording your responses, you send a signal to your brain that you are committed to making this change and are taking the process seriously. Also, by physically recording your thoughts and responses to the questions by hand or digitally, you increase your awareness of your thoughts and feelings to understand them more clearly.

By keeping a record of your responses to the daily five questions, you are also able to look back through them at the end of each week to identify any key themes or patterns. This reflection helps to further deepen your self-awareness, enabling you to become aware of how you've been feeling, what you are focusing on and what you want to achieve. This insight plays an important role in understanding what is driving you, and what gives you energy and where you want to spend your energy.

To make this process easier, you can use the 5Qs template pages at the back of this book to record your responses for each question daily or download the template using the QR code at the back of this book. In this way, you can maintain a digital record and journal of your 5Qs Formula daily.

## Step 4: Highlight relevant sections

As you read, highlight sections of the book that resonate with you or contain key insights. (If reading on an e-reader, you can make use of the highlight and notes functions.) This will make it easier for you to refer back to important information later on.

## Step 5: Familiarise yourself with tools

Pay special attention to the tools introduced in the book, such as the ring of emotions and feelings discussed in chapter 3 and the impact/ urgency grid outlined in chapter 6. Understanding these tools can help you apply the 5Qs Formula seamlessly in your daily life.

## Step 6: Commit to growth

Approach the book with a curious mind and open heart. Commit to your own personal growth and transformation. Understand that by investing time and effort in yourself, you'll not only benefit but also positively impact those around you. Once you know the 5Qs Formula and are familiar with the tools, it will only take you five minutes each day to apply.

## Step 7: Apply the 5Qs Formula daily

Once you have a solid understanding of the 5Qs Formula and have completed the self-reflection exercises, make a commitment to answering each of the 5Qs questions daily. This consistency will help you integrate the 5Qs Formula into your routine and experience its benefits quickly and over time.

Use the PRIME acronym as a memory prompt when you first start out:

**P:** Pinpoint emotions and feelings.

**R:** Recognise gratitude.

**I:** Identify what is working and could be working better.

**M:** Make a list of three high-impact tasks for today.

**E:** Envision how you want to show up today.

# Take advantage of the morning

It's best to apply the 5Qs Formula at the start of your day—before you get consumed by work, jump straight into your first meeting or turn on your laptop. This is because your answers to the questions set the tone for navigating the day ahead. Just like a captain charts the course of a ship before setting sail, engaging in the 5Qs Formula allows you to navigate your day, both personally and professionally, with purpose and clarity.

Remember—you only need to dedicate *five* minutes each morning to completing the 5Qs Formula. This means incorporating the five questions into your morning routine can be done efficiently, even on your busiest days. Also keep in mind pairing the process with existing everyday activities, such as your morning coffee or tea, or commute to work, works well. Even better, combine it with mindfulness practices such as meditation, deep breathing and body scans—these help to centre your focus and create a calm and reflective mindset before taking the questions.

Here are further tips and ideas to make the 5Qs Formula a seamless part of your morning routine:

- *Wake up reflection:* Before getting out of bed, reach over and grab your 5Qs Formula template. Start answering each question and recording your responses.

- *Breakfast check-in:* While preparing or eating breakfast and having your morning tea or coffee, take five minutes to answer your five questions.

- *Mirror moment:* Take five minutes in the bathroom in the morning after washing your face and brushing your teeth to answer each question. Capture your answers in your journal straight after.

- *Set reminders:* Use alarms or notifications on your phone to remind you to do the 5Qs Formula each morning. This will help you ensure you don't forget to prioritise this practice, even on busy days.

- *Keep it simple:* Don't overthink your response to each of the five questions. Trust your instincts and go with whatever comes to mind first. The formula is there to help you develop self-awareness and intentionality, not perfection!

The aim of applying the 5Qs Formula is to intentionally prime your mindset and behaviour for a productive and joyful day. In five minutes each day, you can pause, think, reflect and record your responses to each question. By following these steps and engaging with all the tools I've shared, you'll be well equipped to maximise your daily productivity and fulfilment.

I can't wait for you to experience the transformation I and countless busy individuals have undergone by incorporating the 5Qs Formula into our lives. For many, it has become an indispensable part of their daily routine, described as a personal non-negotiable. My hope is for you to enjoy reading the following chapters, relate to the insights and, most importantly, experience the benefits of productivity joy in your daily life.

# PART II

# The 5Qs Formula

# CHAPTER 3

# Checking your emotional temperature

*Question one: What is your emotional temperature, and what are you feeling today?*

What if acknowledging and labelling your emotions and feelings at the start of the day helped you be more productive, energised and effective each day? Wouldn't you want to learn the simple process to do this? This chapter will help you understand why asking this powerful question as part of the 5Qs Formula will help do just this for you each day.

This first question holds an intentional primacy in the sequence of the formula, because it immediately directs your attention and focus inward, prompting self-awareness and emotional regulation. I've also placed it at the start of the formula because your brain tends to remember things more quickly when they are at the beginning of a list or process, as long as the list or process isn't too long. By checking in with your emotions and feelings at the start of the day, you're more likely to remember to track how you feel as the day progresses, enabling you to manage your emotions promptly so they do not build up and spill over into other aspects of your life.

As I outline in more detail in this chapter, emotions are crucial in decision-making, behaviour, thinking, impact and overall wellbeing. By starting the 5Qs Formula with this question, I'm encouraging you to acknowledge and understand your current emotional state, laying the groundwork for subsequent introspection and action.

This question addresses your inner workings and focuses on your internal landscape. It recognises that above everything else, you are, first and foremost, a human being full of emotions that vibrate and emit and attract energy throughout your day. This influences what you can achieve and how others experience you.

## Understanding the difference between emotions and feelings

Emotions and feelings are often mistaken as the same thing and used interchangeably. Indeed, many adults don't understand the difference between the two, and this is why most of us need to work on developing our emotional intelligence skills. Thankfully, most contemporary schools focus on emotional wellbeing as part of their mainstream education and help children develop their emotional awareness from a young age. This will hopefully lead to future generations of emotionally capable humans with higher levels of emotional intelligence. (Fingers crossed!)

Emotions are your body's language for communicating with you, letting you know about your internal emotional state and how your body is responding to what is going on around you.

Feelings are the brain's language of telling you what your emotions mean, so your emotions make sense to you. Feelings are personal and vary from person to person. For instance, when you experience the emotion of happiness, you may feel excitement, while someone else might feel a sense of calm. Similarly, you may associate feelings such as bitterness, repulsion, shame or horror with the emotion 'disgust', depending on how you perceive a situation. Remember—everyone interprets their emotions differently. Your feelings are your brain's way of making sense of your emotions, which are unique to you.

It's important to remember that emotions and feelings are state-based. This means you are likely to experience various emotions and feelings throughout the day, each of which is neither good nor bad. They will pass; they won't remain permanently. Dr Russ Harris, the pioneer of acceptance and commitment therapy and author of the bestselling *The Happiness Trap*, shares a useful metaphor of 'treating emotions and feelings like clouds; they, too, will pass by'. Just as clouds drift by, emotions arise, linger for a while and eventually dissipate. When you acknowledge that your emotions are transient, they no longer define who you are. Emotions and feelings are not your identity; how you regulate them becomes part of your identity. Treating your emotions as temporary and not becoming overwhelmed or overly attached to a particular emotion allows you to have a more balanced and adaptive response to situations, circumstances and people in your life.

Again, your emotions or feelings do not define who you are. For example, 'I am sad, and I am feeling so pathetic right now, which must mean I am sad and pathetic', is certainly not true. It's essential to be able to step aside from how you feel and recognise that while your emotions and feelings are part of what you are experiencing, they don't define you. In this way, saying, 'I'm feeling pathetic right now, and that's okay; I know it doesn't mean I am pathetic', is a way to use language to help you detach how you talk to yourself about your feelings and emotions. Remember—you will never hear another person's voice more than the voice in your own head! So be intentional and aware of the way you talk to yourself about your emotions and feelings.

## Emotions impact your productivity

Whether you want to acknowledge it or not, emotions influence your experiences, abilities, impact, productivity, concentration levels and overall wellbeing in varying degrees, regardless of your gender identity. Your emotions affect how you think and feel. They affect your cognitive processes by impacting aspects such as how attentive and focused your mind is, and how clearly you can make balanced decisions, solve problems, learn and remember stuff.

For instance, when you're angry or frustrated, you will find it harder to solve problems because you're so focused on what's making you mad. You might also act impulsively without thinking things through. Imagine you are studying for a test or exam. How you feel while studying will affect how well you remember the information later. If you are feeling excited or interested, you're more likely to pay attention, share what you are learning with others, and remember what you are studying. This is because your brain is better at storing information when you're in a good mood.

On the other hand, if you're feeling stressed or upset, it will be harder to concentrate, learn new things and remember what you learnt or did. When you're happy or excited, your brain is like a sponge soaking up water; the learning sticks better. But when you're feeling stressed or upset, it's like trying to soak up water with an already saturated, dripping sponge; it's harder to absorb more water.

When you experience emotions such as happiness or love, these emotions make you feel more motivated, upbeat and full of energy, and they give you a sense that you can take on anything. These emotions make you feel good, optimistic, positive and capable. They provide a sense that you can achieve the things you set out to do. Emotions associated with positive feelings also increase creativity and creative juices, which help you be more innovative and solution-focused. When you are filled with positive feelings, you will notice you come up with different ideas for challenges or problems you are facing.

Emotions play a crucial role in optimising your productivity by channelling your time and energy effectively. When you experience inspiration and joy, your focus sharpens. You will notice your attention stays focused for longer, and you're more likely to put in extra effort to accomplish your task or goal.

Lifestyle aspects such as getting good quality sleep also affect your emotions and feelings and how much you can get done in a day. Take my client Emilia, a parent working from home. When Emilia wakes up feeling refreshed and happy because she has had a night of uninterrupted sleep, she is able to approach her work tasks with energy and enthusiasm. This positive mood helps her stay focused and productive throughout the day, even when performing the tricky job of juggling her work responsibilities while caring for her kids.

Additionally, positive emotions and feelings facilitate meaningful interactions with others, fostering a supportive environment. As I outline through this chapter, your emotions and your ability to regulate them will determine the quality of the relationships you maintain. Building strong relationships not only enhances your sense of fulfilment but also contributes to your productivity. Getting things done is easier when you have the support and the help of others. Everyday accomplishments are rarely achieved in isolation, and they often stem from collaborative efforts and strong support networks.

## *Focus on emotions before tasks and activities*

Just as most adults don't always recognise the difference between an emotion and a feeling, they are also not used to identifying their emotions or, even more so, describing their feelings. Think about this. When you asked someone recently how they are feeling, did they respond with a brief, 'good', 'fine' or 'not bad'?

During your formative years, you were most likely asked about the activities and achievements of your day: 'How was your day?' or 'What did you learn today?' Occasionally, if you were fortunate, you might have been asked a more thoughtful question such as, 'What was the most favourite part of your day?' These enquiries, with their good intentions, will have unintentionally shaped your understanding of meaningful conversation starters. They likely signalled to you a belief that focusing primarily on the accomplishment of daily tasks is what receives recognition and connection with others. Consequently, many adults have developed a habit of prioritising the 'doing' aspect of their lives.

As adults, we find ourselves caught in a pattern of directing our attention towards tasks and activities: 'What are your plans for today?', 'What's been going on?', 'How are things?' However, it's important to remember that you are not merely a 'human doing'—you are a 'human 'being'. Unfortunately, the emphasis on 'doing' often overshadows the essential aspect of your existence—the 'being' dimension, which encompasses your emotional state.

Like most people, no doubt you're busy with multiple responsibilities, stresses and pressures. You rarely have a moment to pause and do your own internal check-in, inquire about your emotional wellbeing, or ask yourself, 'How do I feel today?' This oversight of not checking in with your emotional state may stem from responding to questions along the lines of, 'How was your day? and 'What have you been doing?' during your upbringing. Yet, acknowledging and tending to your emotional self is paramount for your own holistic wellbeing and genuine connection with others.

Question one of the 5Qs Formula taps into your 'being' and encourages you to start your day with an inside–out approach. This question lets you do an internal check-in before you start your day of positive impact, ensuring your emotional compass points in the right direction. Checking your emotional temperature and feelings helps you to align your internal state before facing the external world. For real change, you must first look inward; it's within yourself that profound transformations can truly occur.

## *Introducing the Ring of Emotions*

To really look inside and check your emotional temperature, you need to be able to name your different emotions and feelings. As adults, we experience many different emotions, with different feelings related to these emotions. I've developed my Ring of Emotions (see overleaf) to outline these different emotions and feelings. As shown in the following figure, the Ring of Emotions outlines seven universal emotions and ten feelings linked to these emotions.

All humans can experience the seven emotions included in the Ring of Emotions. Further, these emotions tend to give rise to the following symptoms:

- *Happiness* shows up as smiling, the contraction of facial muscles, especially around the eyes and mouth, and laughing, which involves the contractions of the diaphragm and other muscles in the chest and abdomen. Happiness can also cause an elevated heart rate, because it increases the release of the neurotransmitters serotonin and dopamine. You may notice a relaxed yet upbeat physical state, ease and comfortableness, or increased energy to do things when you experience happiness.

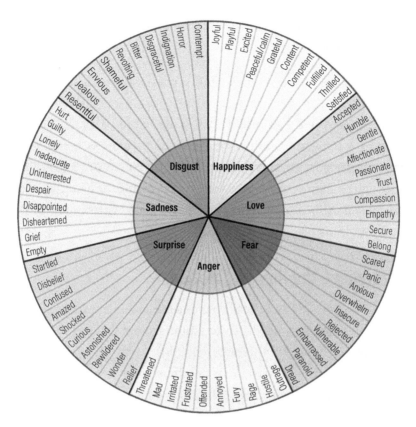

**The Ring of Emotions**

- *Sadness* shows up as crying. Tears usually occur with sniffing or sobbing and/or facial expressions such as a downturned mouth, frowning or a pained expression. You may notice a slump in your posture, drooped or rounded shoulders, slower physical movement, and a downward or distant gaze. Sadness may increase muscle tension, and cause stiff shoulders, neck and jaw, and headaches or migraines. Reduced energy levels, motivation and appetite, or disturbed sleep are also common symptoms of sadness.

- *Love* can fill your stomach with a fluttery sensation, commonly known as 'butterflies', caused by an increased release of hormones such as adrenaline and oxytocin. An increased heart rate, perhaps heart palpations, or a miss of heartbeat, flushed cheeks, dilated pupils, and sweaty palms or forehead are all likely, as well as a warm fuzzy feeling of contentment, calmness and relaxation when around a loved one. When you experience the love emotion, your sensory experiences are heightened; the things you taste, smell, touch, hear and see are more vivid and intense.

- *Anger* can activate the body's fight or flight response, which leads to increased heartbeat and high blood pressure as the body prepares for action. Your muscles will likely tighten and become tense, making your neck, jaw and shoulders stiff. An increased blood flow to your skin's surface can make your face and skin look flushed. Breathing is likely to be shallow and fast, and you may experience shaking or trembling in your hands or legs, as well as clammy palms or sweating. Chronic anger or unresolved anger can also contribute to gastrointestinal problems such as indigestion, acid reflux and irritable bowel syndrome, and to poor-quality sleep.

- *Surprise* can be recognised through specific facial expressions, such as raised eyebrows, a widening of the eyes, and a slightly dropped or open jaw, and through sounds such as a quick gasp or inhalation, and the word 'oh', signalling shock and surprise. You will likely experience a temporary increase in heart rate, blood pressure and skin sensations such as blushing or goosebumps. Due to the initial shock or surprise, you will likely experience a sudden movement such as a jump or a startle reflex, followed by a release of endorphins. This leads to feelings of excitement and amazement if it's perceived as a positive surprise.

- *Disgust* can be identified through specific universal facial expressions such as wrinkling of the nose, lip curling or frowned eyebrows. Intense reactions may include a nausea sensation, an involuntary reaction of gagging or retching, a decreased appetite, shallow or rapid breathing, muscle tension and sweating. Skin reactions, blushing or even becoming pale, as well as 'away' or 'avoidance' behaviours, where you automatically turn away from the offensive stimuli or situation in an attempt to distance yourself from it, are common displays of disgust.

- *Fear* activates the body's flight or fight response, leading to rapid heartbeat as the body prepares to respond to a threat. It can cause rapid or shallow breathing, even hyperventilation, as the body takes in more oxygen to fuel the fight or flight response. This increase in oxygen can cause dizziness or light-headedness. Fear can trigger sweating, trembling or shaking as the body responds to the surge of adrenaline and cortisol. Fear narrows the focus of attention, leading to tunnel vision while dilating your pupils to enhance visual perception of potential threats. Fear will cause dryness in the mouth and throat due to reduced saliva production as the body prioritises all its energy for a fight or flight response.

The more you know about how your body reacts when you experience any of these seven emotions, the more insight and self-awareness you develop about yourself. This awareness helps you know how to regulate your emotions to make them more manageable. In this way, you can use your emotions and feelings to achieve what you need and want to do each day. I provide more detail about how to do this later in this chapter.

## Self-reflection

- Think of a time recently when you have felt one of these seven emotions. Did you feel any of the symptoms or signs associated with the emotion you are reflecting on?

- Take a few moments to reflect and write down what symptoms or signs you felt in your body when you experienced the emotion. While I've provided a general guide, everyone is unique. Therefore, the symptoms of any of the seven emotions may differ slightly for you from how I have described them, which is fine. What's important is being able to identify what symptoms are associated with what emotions for you, so you can start to recognise them as they emerge. Recognising your emotions is the first step to be able to regulate them.

## *Emotions are energy*

Emotions are an energy or vibration you and others can feel inside and with each other. While some people carry stronger emotions than others, all emotions have a charge and distinct frequency associated with them.

Psychiatrist Dr David R Hawkins developed the Emotional Vibration Analysis Frequency Scale, which ranges from lower vibrational emotions such as shame (20) to higher ones such as joy (540), peace (600) and enlightenment (700+). Each person has an overall baseline vibrational frequency at specific times, but experiencing lower vibrational emotions such as shame, guilt, apathy, grief or anger can decrease your frequency. A lower vibrational state can reduce your ability to cope with challenges, making you feel overwhelmed and more reactive. In contrast, maintaining higher vibrational states can significantly improve your interactions with others, because you will radiate more happiness, joy and positivity, thereby positively influencing those around you. You will attract more of what you emit.

By checking your emotional temperature at the start of the day using question one of the 5Qs Formula, you can raise your awareness of your emotional frequency. This awareness allows you to decide if you need or want to change your frequency to better handle the day ahead.

As an example of this, meet my client Sebastian, a seasoned leader at a prominent local authority. He was responsible for a team of 12 direct reports and oversaw a function encompassing 50 individuals. With a tenure of over 15 years, he had climbed the ranks from an assistant officer role, earning a reputation as someone who 'gets things done'. Whether it involved reprimanding an employee, ensuring compliance or driving through necessary changes, Sebastian was the go-to person. While this reputation gave him a sense of importance and authority, Sebastian couldn't shake the awareness that his authoritarian approach instilled fear rather than respect. People would avoid him when they saw him walking down the corridor, or engage in minimal conversations with him. Recognising the need for a transformation, Sebastian sought executive coaching to shift his leadership style from dogmatic to inclusive.

When asked about his motivation for change, Sebastian confessed, 'I know there's a better way to lead, and I want to be able to sleep soundly at night, knowing I've done things right'. Through our coaching sessions, it became apparent that Sebastian's most significant obstacle wasn't external. It was his own fear of losing control and appearing weak that threatened his ego. His ego, driven by this fear, hindered him from embracing inclusive leadership skills such as active listening, collaboration and empowerment. Instead, he resorted to dictating rather than facilitating, inadvertently disempowering those around him and acquiring a reputation deep down he was not proud of.

After this realisation, Sebastian understood that to change how others perceived him he first needed to transform his energy and leadership approach. This epiphany marked the beginning of his journey towards authentic, inclusive leadership, which, at its core, he wanted to be about humility, collaboration and positive impact.

Can you imagine what Sebastian's energy would have been like before he went through his leadership transformation? He hadn't realised his energy was overbearing, intimidating and power-hungry, because he was so focused on getting the job done. With sheer determination, courage and an openness to be vulnerable in his coaching sessions, he was able to learn to shift his energy in line with his leadership aspirations and desired impact.

Have you ever noticed how someone entering a room can seemingly carry a heavy energy of angst, stress and worry into their interactions? This reminds me of when my immediate family teased me by calling me 'the bull'. They said that when I approached them, they felt a metaphorical dark shadow of annoyance and frustration stemming from my tendency to charge into the room, dictating household tasks. Despite my defence that a messy household drove me insane, I failed to realise how my energy was perceived before I even spoke, causing them to tune out. Realising this, I worked on managing my energy, especially when feeling annoyed or frustrated. This approach enabled me to foster cooperation rather than resistance. So if you want to get others onside, it is so important to be aware and show up with the right energy and to notice how others are responding to you.

Remember—we all carry an emotional weather pattern, so it is up to each of us to decide how sunny, bright, dark or cloudy we want ours to be.

Have you ever encountered someone whose immense cheerfulness and upbeat demeanour instantly uplifts and energises you, even in just a few minutes of interaction? This phenomenon occurs because your emotions function like energy, detectable and transferable to others. Psychologists call this 'emotional contagion', where emotions become infectious, spreading among individuals. You may have experienced this at a concert, where the collective excitement electrifies the atmosphere, affecting everyone present.

Emotional contagion holds immense power, with each of us possessing the ability to influence others' emotions. By consciously choosing the emotions you project, you impact those around you. Moreover, the emotions you focus on tend to be the ones that expand and intensify. To cultivate greater joy, fulfilment and energy, it's crucial to focus on positive experiences, nurturing gratitude (as explored in question two in the next chapter) and embracing sources of inspiration and happiness. Directing your attention towards these positive aspects of your life fuels their growth and enhances your wellbeing. Just like a weather pattern, your emotional state attracts similar feelings while repelling unwanted ones from others.

I encourage you to reflect on your emotional states at particular points in your day and ask yourself the following:

- Are you being an emotional radiator—emitting positivity, light, warmth and hope?

- Or are you being an emotional drain—sapping energy, emitting pessimism, negativity and doubt?

The following self-reflection exercise helps you explore this in more detail.

# Self-reflection

Follow these steps to help you work out whether you're being an emotional radiator or not.

1.  Identify a person in your life who is an 'emotional radiator':

    - Notice their energy — do they exude positivity and warmth?

    - What about their outlook on life — do they tend to see the good in situations and people?

    - And their approach to life — do they approach challenges with resilience and optimism?

2.  Identify someone you have come across in your life who has been an 'emotional drain':

    - Notice their energy — do they often seem tired, negative or drained?

    - What about their outlook on life — do they focus more on problems rather than solutions?

    - And their approach to life — do they struggle to cope with challenges and appear pessimistic?

3.  Note the similarities or differences between these two individuals. For example:

    - Similarities could include that both individuals face challenges, but their responses differ.

(*continued*)

- Differences could include emotional radiators tending to maintain a positive outlook, while emotional drains may struggle to find positivity.

4. Consider how you think others would describe you:

   - Do you think others consider you an emotional radiator or an emotional drain?

   - Reflect on your own energy, outlook and approach to life in both your personal and professional life. You may notice you are an emotional radiator or drain in one part of your life and not in the other.

   - Ask yourself — would you want to spend the day with yourself in your current emotional state?

Remember — even if you discover you're not currently an emotional radiator, that's okay. It doesn't define who you are. Awareness is the first step toward change. By implementing the evidence-backed tools in this book, you can start shifting toward emitting positivity and warmth in your interactions and outlook on life. For example, the next time you are in a happy mood, try sharing it with those around you and notice their reactions, the positive impact you have on them and their day.

# Emotional regulation

Meet my client Harsha, a driven and passionate finance director for a multinational financial services firm. She is known for her unwavering commitment to perfectionism. Married to a successful lawyer, she embodies a relentless pursuit of excellence both in her personal and professional life. However, her perfectionism often translates into a rigid leadership style that can be challenging for her team to navigate, especially when disagreements arise.

Recently, Harsha found herself at odds with one of her team members, leaving her feeling frustrated and uneasy. Firm in her convictions and experience, she struggled to accept differing viewpoints, convinced that her way was the only path to achieving the highest standards. Consequently, she took it upon herself to complete the task in question, sacrificing her own personal time and working late into the evening.

The feelings of the disagreement spilt over into their personal life, as Harsha's unresolved emotions led to tension with her husband that evening, and an abrupt run-in with an unfriendly neighbour on her evening walk with her dog. Tensions carried through to the morning, and her usual affectionate farewell to her husband was replaced by silence. All of these moments further exacerbated Harsha's feelings of frustration and isolation.

Her unresolved emotions continued back at the office. They kept her distracted from doing her actual work and lowered her concentration levels, so she took twice as long to read and reply to emails and sign off certain documents. She was scattered in her thoughts and energy. She was physically there, but her mind was not in the present and, instead, she was thinking about the tension between her and her husband. This resulted in more frustration, because she was experiencing a lack of progress in her work and was being unproductive in all she needed to get done that day at work. She approached her team member in another team meeting with defensiveness and impatience. Her communication style, marked with terseness and directness, left her team member feeling upset and somewhat demoralised.

Harsha's situation illustrates the importance of acknowledging and addressing your emotions in a timely manner. Unrecognised or unresolved feelings, when ignored or suppressed, can permeate every aspect of your life, impacting relationships, productivity and overall wellbeing. Recognising emotions and feelings early in the day is crucial, because carrying over unresolved feelings from previous days can hinder your productivity and impact. It's essential to address these feelings promptly to minimise their impact in the shorter and longer term too. Otherwise, bottled up emotions can build up and feel overwhelming, significantly hindering your productivity and overall effectiveness.

By prioritising emotional self-awareness, open communication and not letting yourself feel threatened by others' capabilities or ideas, you can foster healthier relationships at work and home, enabling you to be more productive and magnify your joy.

## Your brain is a 'meaning-making machine'

The human brain is a remarkable meaning-making machine—it loves making sense of things and avoiding uncertainty. It has a natural aversion to ambiguity and the unknown, preferring predictability and familiarity. It craves predictability to keep you safe and healthy. Consequently, the brain appreciates when you seek to acknowledge and label your emotional experiences, because doing so helps the brain create a story of your world, making you feel connected and understood.

The Ring of Emotions I outlined earlier in this chapter helps you accurately identify and label the emotions and feelings you are experiencing each day. By labelling the emotion and feelings, you are acknowledging them. In turn, this helps you reduce the intensity of the emotion and feeling to ensure it serves you to be productive and joyful. By labelling the emotion or feeling, you reduce its power over you and, in this way, your emotions cannot control you—instead, you empower yourself to stay in control of your emotions.

## Acknowledge it, to regulate it

This first question of the 5Qs Formula—What is your emotional temperature, and what are you feeling today?—has been inspired and adapted from the work of Dr Daniel J Siegel and Dr Tina Payne Bryson, who in their fantastic book on parenting, *The Whole-Brain Child*, eloquently share the strategy 'name it, to tame it' as a way to calm big emotions.

While the 'name it, to tame it' strategy is primarily designed for children, I have seen it work exceptionally well with adults of all ages, and especially with my clients. My clients will often hear me say, 'As adults, we are big kids in grown-up bodies!' Emotions are energy; they don't care whether you are big or small. Even as an adult, your emotions continue to react to your internal and external environment, and it's your job to recognise them to control and regulate them. The simplest and most effective way to do this is to acknowledge and label the emotion and feeling you are experiencing. I call this technique, 'acknowledge it, to regulate it'.

At its heart, question one of the 5Qs Formula offers a simple way to 'acknowledge it, to regulate it'—that is, to check in with your emotions and feelings at the start and throughout the day. This enables you to stay connected, positive, fulfilled and energised as you tackle your daily tasks.

Here's a simple three-step process to acknowledge and label your feelings and emotions to help regulate them:

1. *Acknowledge and accept what you are feeling within yourself without any judgment.* For example, 'I feel mad and angry at

how my partner spoke to me', or 'I feel frustrated that my colleague cannot see things from a different perspective'.

2. *Give the emotion and feeling a label.* Using the Ring of Emotions from earlier in this chapter, label your emotions and feelings. Doing so can help you recognise and acknowledge the emotion or feeling more clearly and help you to reduce its intensity so it doesn't control you.

3. *Validate what you feel.* Remind yourself that it's okay to feel the way you do. No emotions and feelings are right or wrong, good or bad, so try not to judge yourself for feeling a certain way. You are entitled to experience and interpret them as you do. Accepting and validating them without judgment will help you process them more effectively, and so find it easier to regulate their hold on you. Think of it like needing to be heard before truly listening or seeking respect before it's earned. Once you validate your feelings — listen to and respect them — you can then focus on understanding and regulating them more effectively.

I recall facilitating a workshop on being an 'active ally' for about 50 leaders and managers for a global manufacturing firm. I emphasised the importance of showing up for your team and genuinely demonstrating that they matter. During the session, one leader shared his recent experience during his paternity leave. His manager and team regularly checked in on him while he was away, asking about his wellbeing, his baby and his wife, and offering support. He revealed that the transition to fatherhood, with sleepless nights and supporting his partner, was taking a toll on him. However, these informal yet thoughtful check-ins had made him feel seen, recognised and valued.

As other leaders in the room listened, I noticed nods of agreement and a shift in the room's energy. Arms uncrossed, and the atmosphere became more connected, supportive and compassionate. Creating space for people to acknowledge and share what's really going on for them can help them feel lighter for having shared, reassured that they've been understood and confident they are supported.

Remember, emotions are a natural part of being human and serve as signals that something is happening internally. Acknowledging and managing your emotions from the beginning of your day, and then consistently throughout, will improve your focus on essential tasks, increase productivity and allow you to impact others positively. This emotional self-awareness is a great way to manage your daily stress levels and improve overall physical and psychological wellbeing.

## *Productive versus unproductive emotions*

If you haven't already experienced them, you'll likely encounter the seven different emotions from the Ring of Emotions at some point in your life. Despite their varying nature, even emotions such as anger and fear can prove beneficial if effectively managed, allowing you to channel them towards calm and assertive responses.

For example, you may encounter a situation that triggers anger, such as witnessing someone being mistreated. Your anger may empower you to assertively stand up for yourself or others facing injustice. Similarly, if a neighbour or friend crosses a personal boundary, your anger might prompt you to establish healthier boundaries in your relationships and interactions with them.

Experiencing fear can help you act more carefully and approach a potentially risky situation with caution and prudence. Fear triggers the body's fight or flight response, which helps you react quickly to potential threats of danger, such as a home intrusion or rescuing someone in distress in a pool.

Awareness of your emotional state and its impact on your actions and behaviours is key to managing your productivity. When stress and anxiety start leading to feelings of annoyance, frustration or even paralysis, it's a sign that they're no longer serving their purpose. At this point, managing and mitigating these overwhelming emotions is essential in order to be productive and take care of your wellbeing. Later in this chapter, I outline three effective strategies to help you change your emotional states when your emotions and feelings are overwhelming and are not serving you. (See the section 'Move, breathe, visual expansion—three science-backed hacks'.)

Understanding the delicate balance between stress and motivation is crucial, because it helps you discern when stress shifts from being beneficial to detrimental. A moderate level of stress, anxiety and pressure can motivate you into action to complete a task, work toward a goal or deliver an assignment on time. This is described well by Robert Yerkes and John Dodson, who discovered a 'sweet spot' of pressure, where productivity thrives. According to Yerkes and Dodson, when pressure is too low, inertia sets in and you likely won't act, resulting in decreased productivity. On the other hand, excessive pressure leads to stress, which also leads to reduced productivity. Similarly, when fear becomes overwhelming, it ceases to be productive and instead becomes counterproductive.

Over time, stress and fear will manifest as an annoyance, frustration or even paralysis, potentially inducing procrastination. You may even feel down about yourself, lose your confidence, and even give up and not complete a task or goal you set out to do. Therefore, being aware of your emotions is key to making sure they help you instead of hinder you in reaching your goals.

When emotions become overbearing, they can affect your self-esteem and confidence. Remember, your goal here is not only to accomplish your daily tasks and objectives, but also to ensure that the process is sustainable, joyful and conducive to your wellbeing. By prioritising the 5Qs Formula at the beginning of your day, you are proactively prioritising self-care and effectively managing stress levels. This approach helps you maintain your confidence, self-esteem and motivation to achieve your goals, even when faced with challenges.

When emotions are heightened, they can become overwhelming and control your thinking and your actions, potentially causing harm to yourself and others. In 2012, while living in Melbourne with my husband before having children, I experienced a terrifying ordeal during a bushfire. Driving back from a client meeting on a scorching 42-degree day, I noticed a distant fire in a field near the freeway. As I drove, the fire rapidly approached, engulfing the roadside in flames and obscuring my vision with smoke and ash. In my complete panic, I made a rash decision to open my car window, only to fill the car with smoke. Feeling trapped and terrified, I was not sure what to do. I slowly inched the car forward not knowing what was ahead of me, pressing the horn rampantly. (I thought if other drivers also couldn't see anything, at least they might be able to hear the horn.) I then saw another car, driven by a woman who had turned her car in the opposite direction, but was on the same side of the freeway as me. She looked extremely panicked and she yelled, 'We need to get out of here'. As sirens blared and a helicopter hovered overhead, a miracle happened.

At that very moment, a man in a white van pulled his car next to mine and reassuringly said, 'We need to tailgate each other and get off at the next junction; come behind me and follow my van'. He yelled over to the other driver and instructed her to turn her car back around and follow behind mine. We followed his instructions and thankfully, with his guidance, made it off the freeway to safety. The fire was finally controlled before reaching a nearby petrol station. This was definitely the most harrowing experience of my life and, reflecting on it, it made me question my action of opening the car window in the middle of a blazing fire. When emotions were high, my judgement was literally clouded and hijacked by my fight or flight response, which led to a risky decision in the moment of crisis.

During periods of intense pressure, stress or perceived threats such as tight deadlines, challenging conversations or in moments of crisis similar to the one I just shared, emotions can escalate, leading to what psychologists term the 'hijacked amygdala' phenomenon. In this state, the brain's emotion centre overrides rationality, leading to impulsive and out-of-character behaviour. You don't see anything or think beyond your immediate focus, as tunnel vision and narrow thinking take over. A notable example is the altercation between two of my favourite celebrities, Chris Rock and Will Smith, on 27 March 2022 at the 94th Academy Awards, where Will Smith walked onstage and slapped comedian Chris Rock across the face in response to a joke Rock made about Will's wife, Jada Pinkett Smith. Will Smith's loss of emotional control damaged his reputation, credibility and popularity. Unchecked emotions or lack of emotional regulation can lead to an amygdala hijack, which can have significant consequences on both your personal and professional fronts.

The more you are aware of your emotions and the symptoms you experience, the more adept you become at controlling your emotions in stressful situations rather than allowing them to control you and dictate your behaviour.

Being aware of changes in your body, and how these might affect your emotions, is also important. For women, the effects of fluctuating hormones can sometimes lead to erratic emotions, whether due to your menstrual cycle, perimenopause or menopause. I've found that implementing the morning emotional temperature check-in is a compassionate way to navigate yourself through these phases of life. Despite the havoc hormones may wreak, intentionally tuning into your emotions, acknowledging and labelling them, empowers you to regulate their impact on your thoughts and feelings. This allows you to consciously choose how you'll respond to the day ahead.

## Emotional intelligence is a critical skill

After coaching numerous executives and leaders, it is clear to me that emotional intelligence is a distinguishing factor of impactful and inspiring leadership. Leaders with high emotional intelligence are a joy to work for and collaborate with. Consequently, their teams will readily move mountains to support them.

Effective leaders not only demonstrate high intellectual intelligence but also excel in recognising and regulating emotions, both within themselves and others. They connect authentically with their team, fostering loyalty and collaboration. This genuine connection serves as a catalyst, motivating their team to achieve exceptional results and fostering a culture of high performance and deep engagement. Within this environment, individuals experience heightened levels of satisfaction, joy and fulfilment. They feel not only recognised but also valued, knowing that their contributions truly make a difference. This transcends beyond mere belonging, it embodies a sense of significance and purpose.

Possessing high levels of emotional intelligence is not solely beneficial in the corporate world, either; it's also a valuable life skill that can make a significant difference to various aspects of your life, whether as a business owner, parent, sibling, friend or student.

My client Josephine, a devoted working mother who cherishes her children and is passionate about her role as a general practitioner at her local surgery, provides an excellent example here. Through her journey, she has learnt the benefits of emotional awareness and emotional regulation, enabling her to recognise her own feelings and better understand her reactions to her children's behaviours.

Now equipped with these skills, Josephine responds to her children's needs with calmness and compassion rooted in empathy and understanding. She proactively manages her stress before interacting with her children, ensuring that her interactions are positive and constructive, even during overwhelming moments. By incorporating the 5Qs Formula into her daily routine, Josephine has noticed a tangible shift in her household dynamics—including less shouting and nagging, and more positive interactions with her children. She observes her children becoming more open and expressive about their emotions and feelings, as they learn to navigate them effectively.

Remember—children learn by watching and observing what you do. By learning to implement the 5Qs Formula, as Josephine did, you too, if you have dependents, can teach them through role-modelling the valuable skills of emotional intelligence that will serve them throughout their lives. When children see their parents and caregivers acknowledging and healthily expressing their feelings, they learn to do the same.

It's important to note that leadership is not about titles and status; it's about positively influencing others, whether at work, at home with your family, or in other parts of your personal life. By understanding and managing your emotions and connecting authentically with others, you can inspire trust, collaboration and productivity, and make yourself and others feel great at the same time. In every aspect of your life, emotional intelligence empowers you to lead effectively and show up to make a positive and meaningful impact on yourself or those around you.

## Responding rather than reacting

Real harm can result when you do not regularly acknowledge and validate your emotions and feelings. Ignoring or dismissing your emotions can lead to suppression, where you push your feelings down instead of processing them. When you do not acknowledge and validate your emotions, it's like vigorously shaking a fizzy drink bottle without releasing the pressure. As the pressure builds up inside the bottle, it becomes increasingly volatile and unstable. Similarly, when suppressed or ignored, emotions accumulate, similar to the pressure inside the bottle, leading to emotional turbulence and potential explosions. Just as gently and regularly releasing the cap of the fizzy drink bottle allows the pressure to be released, by acknowledging and validating your emotions, you prevent them from reaching a point of explosion and causing harm to yourself and others. Instead, you provide a safety measure, a release valve for the built-up tension within you.

In this way question one of the 5Qs Formula, asks you to check your emotional temperature, helps you develop the habit of responding rather than reacting to your day, circumstances, responsibilities and the people around you.

I'm sure you've experienced the difference between reacting and responding to situations and the people around you. Perhaps a driver hasn't given way to you at a junction, or a direct report is spending way too long explaining something to you, or the technology you are using today is not functioning properly?

When you are busy, tired, or the pressure is on and time is of the essence, it can be so easy to fall into the trap of becoming reactive to these types of situations and those around you, and even yourself. You have less patience, and are short, snappy, on the attack or the defence, and quick to blame or justify. When you react, you surrender your agency to something or someone external to you. You'll notice your behaviour is impulsive, rushed and unclear, and your tone of voice may come across as demeaning, impatient and even belittling. I'm sure this is not the impact you'd be hoping to have.

Alternatively, when you respond, you're actively making a deliberate choice about how you'll behave and what you'll say. This intentional approach preserves your self-agency, enabling you to stay measured, composed and balanced. Ultimately, responding rather than reacting empowers you to exert control over your actions, fostering a calmer and more positive impact on both yourself and others.

A practical yet simple technique to help you respond rather than react is to implement a strategic pause, which acts like a momentary circuit breaker. Take a few seconds or perhaps, if time allows, a minute or two. This is a moment to reflect before deciding or responding to a situation.

When you implement the strategic pause, ask yourself this helpful question: how can I respond in a way that aligns with my values and the impact I want to have? When you get into a habit of using a strategic pause to ask yourself this question, you'll notice you are more in control, calmer and measured. You will be far less reactive, much more productive and also feel more satisfied and positive about yourself.

This approach also conveys to others that you are emotionally stable, rational, grounded and considerate. When others feel this way in your presence, they know they can rely on the consistency of your behaviours and feel confident that, whatever the situation, you will respond in a balanced and measured manner. This helps them feel safe to be themselves when around you.

## Move, breathe, visual expansion — three science-backed hacks

If you notice that your emotional state is not going to help you achieve what you need and want to achieve on a given day, you can apply one or all of the following MBV—or move, breath and visual expansion—strategies. These three simple science-backed hacks help you shift your emotional state into a positive one, so you can achieve what you need to do on a given day.

Here's how to adopt a MBV strategy:

1. *Move:* Physical movement, such as stretching your arms out, standing up and stretching your legs, running on the spot, star jumps or dancing, even for only one or two minutes, will instantly shift your emotions into feeling more joyful, happy and uplifted through the release of endorphins. You could put on your favourite song and sing along or dance to it, which will also help you feel more joyful and liberated.

2. *Breathe:* Neuroscientist Dr Andrew Huberman shares compelling research on the benefits of a particular type of breathing, which includes taking two short, quick inhale breaths in through your nose, followed by one long exhale breath out through your mouth. Practising this breathing exercise for as little as three to four breaths will help you feel calmer and more relaxed because it activates the body's parasympathetic relaxation system, which minimises the nerves or anxiety you may be feeling.

3. *Visual expansion:* When stressed, your brain is often reacting to fear, triggering a flight or fight response. Staring at screens or focusing narrowly and intensely can make this worse. Instead, try expanding or widening your vision. Imagine standing on

a balcony or at the top of a hill, taking in a wide, expansive view. You can do this by physically stepping outside or looking out of your window, far and wide. This activates your peripheral vision, signalling to your brain that you are safe and can relax. Just take a few minutes to look into the distance, and you will instantly feel calmer.

# Applying the 5Qs Formula: Question one

Question one of the 5Qs Formula asks you to check in on your emotional temperature, and what you are feeling today. Your emotions and feelings only need one thing: to be acknowledged. Just as a child seeks comfort and understanding from a parent, your emotions long to be recognised and embraced by your inner caregiver. When you acknowledge and validate your feelings, you provide yourself with the nurturing support needed to be productive and you take care of your wellbeing. Like a parent comforts their child's sadness, or as a gardener tends to their plants, tending to your emotions with care and compassion nurtures your inner growth, bringing out the best in you and what you can achieve.

Recognising and acknowledging your feelings at the start of the day is a proactive step to identifying any stress and anxiety you may be experiencing. In this way, you are likely to avoid experiencing chronic stress or anxiety—because you are identifying how you feel along the way, before your emotions escalate out of control. You are also setting yourself up to experience productivity joy, because you can adjust and change your emotional state once you are aware of it.

By assessing your emotional temperature each morning, you can better understand how you feel throughout the day and adjust your work, studies or day routine accordingly. For example, if you check in and realise you're feeling particularly energised, you might tackle more challenging tasks first, whereas if you're feeling overwhelmed, you might prioritise your tasks accordingly. Asking yourself this first question can also help you realise if anything from the previous days is still bothering you or influencing your mood and demeanour.

The simplest way to answer question one of the 5Qs Formula each morning is to look at the Ring of Emotions from earlier in this chapter and identify which of the seven emotions best describes how you feel that morning.

To do this, first tune into what you're feeling in your body by briefly pausing, closing your eyes, and bringing your attention inward. Notice what your body is feeling, such as butterflies or nervousness, and doing, such as slouched shoulders or a wrinkled nose. Use the list provided earlier in this chapter (refer to the section 'Introducing the Ring of Emotions) to familiarise yourself with the common symptoms for each of the seven emotions.

Once you have identified the primary emotion you are experiencing that morning, move to the outer circle and identify which of the ten 'feeling' labels best represents your current feelings. You may choose multiple feeling labels to describe how you feel at the start of the day.

Remember the key to this part of the 5Qs Formula is to simply recognise and acknowledge your emotional state, rather than ignoring, dismissing or dwelling on it. While you may take this opportunity to ask yourself why you may be feeling the way you do and to connect your feelings to a specific cause, person, situation, event or incident, this next level of curiosity is not essential to get the benefits of simply acknowledging your emotions. Becoming overly curious about why you feel a particular way could slow down the action you need to take to progress with your day. Remember, feelings and emotions are not fixed; they will change as you progress through the day. The most important aspect at this point is that you have recognised and acknowledged your initial emotional state.

You might be too preoccupied in the morning to contemplate your feelings or perhaps reluctant to dwell on them, fearing doing so might exacerbate your distress. A helpful strategy is to still acknowledge your emotions and feelings but then designate a specific 'worry time' to dive into them—perhaps at 8 pm in the evening. If you still experience the same emotions by then, you can use this time to delve into your feelings and reflect on their underlying causes. Simply by setting aside this designated time, you signal to your brain that you acknowledge and respect your emotions, and promise to address them later if they persist. Often, you'll discover that by the time the designated 'worry time' comes around, your emotions and feelings no longer trouble you as intensely.

Therefore, the key to this question is to take your emotional temperature by simply acknowledging your emotions and feelings and, in this way, create a baseline of your emotional state at the start of your day. You might feel angry and furious about an upcoming situation you have to handle. Acknowledging that you feel this way will help the intensity of the anger subside, meaning you are less likely to let the anger control or take over when you handle the situation.

Question one of the 5Qs Formula enables you to validate and acknowledge your feelings and emotions so they don't go unrecognised, unvalidated and unacknowledged, and so build up into something bigger than they need to be. Remember, your emotions and feelings are a part of your experience, but they do not define who you are and what you can achieve.

By acknowledging and labelling your emotions and feelings at the start of your day, you've shown yourself care, consideration and kindness, which means you can focus on achieving the best of the day.

# Summary

Emotions and feelings are central to all human beings; in this way, they should not be ignored, dismissed or discounted, because doing so will only mean they intensify or build up. They are part of you and must be acknowledged and managed. When you can recognise, acknowledge and manage your emotions and feelings daily, you will be more productive by achieving more, being more focused and attentive, and feeling more positive, fulfilled and energised. Taking your emotional temperature each day helps you set yourself and your day up for greater success and impact.

# Key takeaways

- Emotions are your body's language of communicating with you. They let you know about your internal emotional state and how your body responds to the world around you.

- Feelings are the brain's language of telling you what your emotions mean, so your emotions make sense to you.

- Your emotions affect how you think and feel. They affect your cognitive processes by affecting aspects such as how sharp your mind is, and how well you can focus, make decisions, solve problems, and learn and remember information.

- Recognising and acknowledging emotions and feelings is vital in helping you be more productive with your time and energy.

- Emotions and feelings need to be labelled to make it easier to regulate them — acknowledge it, to regulate it.

- The Ring of Emotions helps you quickly identify and label your emotions and feelings each day, allowing you to focus on your day in the best way possible.

- Acknowledging your feelings at the start of the day is a proactive step to identifying any stress and anxiety you may be experiencing, enabling you to implement timely coping strategies and building emotional resilience throughout the day.

- By taking your emotional temperature each day, you set yourself and your day up for success, enabling you to respond (rather than react) to your day, situations, projects, tasks and interactions.

# CHAPTER 4

# Gratitude shapes your brain

*Question two, part A: What experiences, things or people in your life are you grateful for because they inspire you to be a better version of yourself?*

*Question two, part B: Think of a time you have received gratitude and appreciation from someone; how did it make you feel?*

Question two (parts A and B) of the 5Qs Formula is an explicit tool to hack or uplift your mood at the beginning of your day. When you express gratitude or recall instances of receiving it, your brain releases positive, feel-good chemicals, fostering a sense of self-worth. This instils within you a greater belief in your capabilities, boosts your confidence and cultivates a mindset of 'I can do this'. Consequently, these initial feelings of positivity have the power to drive and motivate you to tackle your tasks throughout your day, even those that seem complex and challenging, and energise you to accomplish them. Remember—the first step of starting a task is often the hardest. Question two serves as a powerful catalyst, propelling you past hesitation and self-doubt into a proactive momentum, setting the tone for a productive day ahead.

# Defining gratitude

Gratitude is all about being thankful, giving thanks, and acknowledging your appreciation for something, someone, a situation or an experience. This includes acknowledging and being thankful to yourself as well as to others. Without gratitude, life feels hollow and dark.

Genuine appreciation enriches your life and connections, infusing warmth and significance into each day. It highlights the fortunes in your life and communicates to others the value, respect and deep appreciation you hold for them. Gratitude fulfils a fundamental human need to belong. Your sense of belonging is maintained when you believe yourself and others you care about matter and feel valued, appreciated and cared for.

Feeling like you matter is important. Professor Gordon Flett from York University in Toronto highlights that when someone feels like they matter, they feel a personal sense of significance, which makes them feel important, visible and heard. On the contrary, when someone feels like they do not matter to others, they experience feelings of unimportance, invisibility and being unheard. Gratitude helps to signal to others that what they do and who they are matters.

At its very core, gratitude illuminates kindness, love and care, nurturing meaningful relationships and reciprocity in your interactions. It imbues these interactions with depth, intimacy and impact, enriching the bonds you share.

Being grateful is a mindset that can be developed and strengthened, so it becomes a way of thinking, interacting and being—essentially, a way of living and showing up in your daily life.

You can express, acknowledge and find gratitude in the following ways:

- *Expressing:* This is when you show appreciation to someone for their generosity, kindness, time, guidance or support through your words or actions. This act makes the receiver feel recognised, valued and appreciated, and brings you as much joy as the receiver. When was the last time you expressed thanks to someone? Can you remember what it felt like for you?

- *Acknowledging:* This is when you take the time to reflect on and appreciate all the positive aspects of your life, including the people, things and experiences you are thankful for. Every person has fortunes, blessings and privileges in their life; you may just need to search deeper to seek them out at certain times or phases in your life. Once you start to see them, you'll start to see more of them. In some ways, the human brain works quite simplistically; if you let it know what you're searching for, it won't stop till it finds it. For example, when you're looking to buy a specific car, do you keep noticing that same car everywhere you go? In the same way, by acknowledging your fortunes, you intentionally prompt your brain to select, actively search for and notice all the fortunes in your life, even the smallest. What fortunes come to mind for you?

- *Discovering nature:* When you are out in nature, taking a simple walk in the rainforest, woods or around a lake, cycling through the hills, or being close to the ocean, you have an opportunity to take in the majestic beauty of nature.

Knowing your environment and awakening your five senses (sight, hearing, touch, smell and taste) to appreciate and connect with your surroundings is a great way to enjoy and show gratitude to nature and wonderful Mother Earth. When was the last time you did this? Do you have an opportunity to spend time in nature in the coming days or weeks, even for just a short while?

- *Embracing the present:* When you fully embrace an experience at hand, you pause to immerse yourself in what you're observing, feeling and appreciating about that moment. One cherished memory stands out vividly in my mind: an afternoon during the school holidays spent with my then nine-year-old son. As we strolled down a bustling high street en route to the cinema, he reached out for my hand and kept hold of it, chattering away to me, even as other youngsters passed us by. I wondered whether he'd let go, thinking he was too cool to hold his mother's hand, but to my surprise, we continued walking and talking, hand in hand. Being a mother of two young boys, I embraced that precise moment and held onto its specialness, knowing it's a memory I want to treasure and not take for granted. As he grows up, those moments of public affection from him will inevitably become fewer. Undoubtedly, you too have your own memories, moments of profound appreciation that you long to treasure forever. Take a moment to observe what memories come up for you. It may even be a moment you experience as you read this book.

- *Showing kindness:* This is all about paying it forward and being thankful for the opportunity to help others in need. I specifically recall an evening when I rushed to the supermarket with my eldest son to grab some last-minute items for dinner. On reaching the checkout, I realised in a panic that I had left my purse at home. The customer next in line, realising what had happened, asked the cashier how much my shopping was, and quickly pulled out her credit card and paid for my shopping. Despite my initial reluctance to accept a stranger's generosity, she insisted, refusing to take my details for reimbursement. Instead, she simply said, 'You can thank me by paying it forward to someone else in need'. This was a wonderful lesson for my son and me to witness together and learn from. Acts of kindness serve as reminders of the positive, caring gestures that occur daily within humanity.

Whether you directly experience being on the receiving end of acts of kindness, or you hear of them happening to others, it instantly lifts your mood and inspires you to extend kindness to others. Take a moment to reflect on how you feel after reading about this woman's act of kindness. Does it evoke memories of other acts of kindness you've experienced as well?

## *Changing your wiring*

Interestingly, most people, including myself, must intentionally and deliberately practice and develop a gratitude mindset, because it won't come naturally. The human brain isn't hardwired for gratitude; instead, it's predisposed to focus on negative aspects, a phenomenon psychologists call the brain's 'negativity bias'. Given the brain's remarkable intelligence—and adaptability—you might wonder why this is the case. The answer lies in the evolution of the human brain, right back to our primal ancestors. In those ancient times, survival depended on being constantly vigilant for threats and dangers. The brain's primary function was to detect anything negative that could jeopardise life and limb. This primal instinct served to protect early humans from predators such as sabre-toothed tigers, which posed a constant threat. Consequently, the human brain evolved to filter out information unrelated to immediate survival, and today still keeps you hyper-focused on avoiding risks and ensuring your safety. This means the brain's default mode prioritises threat detection and risk avoidance, rather than focusing on positive aspects. This is why cultivating a gratitude mindset requires conscious and intentional effort in a world vastly different from our ancestral environment.

Thankfully, in today's world, you do not need to worry about being eaten by a sabre-toothed tiger. However, other fears and distractions will no doubt consume your brain's time, energy and focus, in a similar way to avoiding the sabre-toothed tiger. These fears and distractions may include feelings such as overwhelm, stress, dissatisfaction, inadequacy, the pressure of juggling multiple priorities, a lack of time, self-critical thinking and self-doubt, unrealistic expectations, letting others down, comparison and despair, grief, loss or trauma, mental health conditions, worrying or being concerned about the future, a lack of self-confidence, and a lack of support or mentorship. These perceived distractions and challenges can make it harder for you to focus on the more positive aspects of your life, the ones you are most grateful for.

## Self-reflection

What do you think gets in the way of you being grateful? Is it time, competing demands, juggling multiple responsibilities, a negative outlook, or a combination of reasons? This is an important question to ask yourself. Once you recognise what your potential blockers could be to practising gratitude, you will be better positioned to do something about it and apply this aspect of the formula more effectively.

Remember, you can only change what you are aware of. It's common to get stuck in your own way and become the bottleneck of your own growth and development. When you don't take the time to fully understand what you are experiencing and what is going on for you, nothing will change for you. However, through a few moments of self-reflection on a question such as this, you will realise what you may need to change to help you cultivate a habit of gratitude in your life.

## Understanding the science and benefits of gratitude

Practising gratitude can get de-prioritised in both your personal life and your professional life for many reasons. I totally get it; when you're busy, life gets in the way! However, I really don't want you to miss out on the immense benefits of gratitude, which include psychological, mood-related, motivational and social benefits, resilience and mental wellbeing. Strong evidence demonstrates that practising gratitude significantly benefits you, regardless of whether you are a leader, manager, business owner, parent, professional or student. The benefits become even greater than just for yourself, extending to those you interact with, work alongside, lead, manage, care for and love.

Have you noticed how good it makes you feel when someone shares how thankful they are for something you did? You can't help but smile or perhaps blush. Knowing that your actions have been noticed and have positively affected someone else can make you feel valued and acknowledged. It's a tangible validation that what you did matters to them and, most importantly, you made a meaningful difference to them. Similarly, when you express to someone how much their actions have positively affected you and helped you, it fosters similar feelings in the other person. Assisting others not only brings personal fulfilment but also reinforces your core values, fostering a positive self-image internally and in the eyes of others.

I recently provided a verbal reference to a recruitment agency on behalf of one of my casual team members. I would have loved for her to continue working with me, but I was unable to offer her the full-time employment she was seeking. I was honoured to provide an authentic endorsement of her capabilities and the significant impact she had made during her time with me. Soon after, she excitedly informed me that she had been offered the role. Her gratitude overflowed through numerous calls and messages, which reflected her elation and appreciation. Witnessing her joy and knowing I had played a part in facilitating her career advancement filled me with immense happiness, too. As humans, we realise at our core that serving humanity is a primal act; we empathise when someone is hurt, needs help or risks their own existence to save others. We believe in a bigger cause than just ourselves.

But what's the science behind this? Expressing or receiving gratitude lights up two key regions in the brain called the medial prefrontal cortex and the anterior cingulate cortex. These regions play a crucial role in processing and regulating your mood and feelings of happiness and positive wellbeing, as identified by Antonio Damasio, the world-class cognitive neuroscientist. Neuroimaging studies have shown that when you express or receive gratitude, these regions in the brain are stimulated, and they release dopamine, the neurotransmitter associated with reward and motivation.

When you experience increased dopamine levels, the behaviours of expressing or receiving gratitude become reinforced. When any behaviour is positively reinforced, it is very likely to be repeated. An example of this is Janina, a maths teacher who spent extra time helping a struggling student understand a difficult concept. Eventually, her student grasped the concept, and he expressed his sincere gratitude for his teacher's assistance. This expression of gratitude triggered a dopamine release in Janina's brain, leading to feelings of satisfaction that she had made a difference to the student. As a result, Janina became more inclined to continue offering extra help to students in need because the positive reinforcement of gratitude strengthened her ability to provide support and guidance. Both her and her students continued to benefit immensely in numerous ways, in addition to becoming better at maths, from her extra support.

When you experience the dopamine release after you receive gratitude, you are likely to help others even more, because your brain enjoys the dopamine hit and so you find it satisfying and rewarding—just as Janina did. You can build your momentum of experiencing dopamine hits through practising and cultivating gratitude into your habitual behaviours—creating a 'gratitude habit' that keeps gifting to yourself and to others.

Studies have shown that gratitude also activates the hypothalamus, an area in the brain responsible for regulating stress levels. When the hypothalamus is activated, it reduces the body's stress response system by reducing the release of cortisol (a stress hormone), which alleviates anxiety and stress. In turn, the body's parasympathetic (relaxation) system becomes activated, making you feel safe and calm.

The neurotransmitter serotonin is also released from a cluster of nuclei in the brain stem called the raphe nucleus and from a few other places in the brain when gratitude is received or expressed. Serotonin leaves you feeling happy, which promotes positive wellbeing.

Studies have shown that individuals who regularly engage in gratitude exercises, such as keeping a gratitude journal or expressing thanks to others, have higher serotonin levels and experience greater overall satisfaction. People with higher serotonin levels are often more resilient to stress and better able to cope with personal and professional challenges. By practising gratitude correctly, as detailed further in this chapter, you, too, will experience the benefits of increased serotonin and dopamine levels.

As an added bonus, the Mayo Clinic Health System has also noted that gratitude is linked to better sleep, improved mood and enhanced immunity. This means those who practise gratitude regularly have higher quality of sleep, more positive mood and can fight off colds, flus and other ailments more quickly, or with reduced disruption to their everyday life.

# Going beyond identifying what you are grateful for

Recent research, shared by leading neuroscientist Dr Andrew Huberman, highlights that when you receive gratitude, you actually get a bigger dopamine hit than when you express gratitude to others. Simply put, being genuinely thanked and appreciated by others gives you a far more significant psychological boost of positivity than when you thank others.

I'm not advocating here that you do not practise giving thanks to others and expressing your gratitude, because this is also essential to help you build reciprocal, mutually respected and meaningful relationships with others. People are likely to want to help you and support you again when they know you appreciate their effort, time and energy. Therefore, it's important to acknowledge them and ensure they feel appreciated too. Similarly, and linked to the law of reciprocity, as humans, we feel indebted to help those who help us or those that we feel close to. So when you express gratitude to others, it reinforces their behaviour of continuing to help where possible. In this way, individually and collectively, you help yourself and others live with purpose and intention, which leads to greater levels of collective productivity and joy.

Gratitude, in fact, strengthens social bonds and relationships because it activates regions of the brain associated with social bonding and interpersonal feelings, which foster connection, empathy and increased overall wellbeing. Expressing and receiving gratitude will help you form strong, meaningful relationships with others. Please remember that gratitude always needs to be genuine and sincere. You can't fake it, because it won't have the impact you intended on the other person, and it won't give you the dopamine and serotonin boost you were hoping for either. I often say to my clients that everyone has a BS meter, and can easily sniff out when someone is not being honest or is disingenuous. Therefore, when you express gratitude to others—or receive gratitude—it's essential to be sincere, genuine and authentic. Additionally, the emotions you experience from gratitude are contagious. As mentioned in chapter 3, psychologists call this transfer of emotions 'emotional contagion'. This means the positive emotions you experience can quickly be passed on to others, creating a positive ripple effect that reaches far beyond those in your immediate sphere.

Interestingly, Dr Huberman's recent research questions the validity of current gratitude practices, which tend to focus on journaling or writing down what you are grateful for. In fact, when I first started developing my 5Qs Formula, the gratitude component of the formula asked you to do just this. Many of my clients would respond to question two in this way and notice they experienced an initial uplift in mood. However, over time—during the course of the day and the course of weeks they committed to implementing the initial formula—the impact of how they felt when writing down what they were grateful for was no longer as strong or noticeable.

So I started to test Dr Huberman's premise that receiving gratitude was more powerful. I asked my clients to focus on recalling a time when they had received gratitude from others—and their self-reported measures ended up supporting Dr Huberman's research. They, too, reported higher levels of positive mood and greater levels of motivation when thinking about the times they had received gratitude from others. It was based on this research that I further developed question two of the 5Qs Formula to what it is now. So if you really want to reap the dopamine benefits of practising gratitude, you need to go beyond simply reminding yourself of what you are grateful for and respond to both parts A and B of question two of the 5Qs Formula.

If you are unable to remember a time when you have received gratitude from someone else for what you did and how you helped them, you can remind yourself of a story when someone else has received help from another. This, too, has been shown to have similar dopamine release effects on the brain.

A story that really still gives me goosebumps every time I recall it is Derek Redmond's emotional story of his race during the 1992 Barcelona Olympics. He was competing in the 400-metre semi-final when, halfway through, he tore his hamstring and fell to the ground in agony. Despite the injury, he was determined to finish the race. Instead of giving up, he struggled up and hobbled forward, the pain etched on his face. Then out of the blue, his father, Jim Redmond, ran onto the track to help his son. Together, they completed the remaining distance, with Derek leaning on his father for support among the cheers and tears from the crowd. Though Derek didn't win the gold medal, this moment was not just about athletics; it was about love, resilience and the unbreakable bond between a father and his son. You can only imagine how deeply grateful Derek would have felt for his father's love, support and commitment in his moment of desperation and vulnerability.

Reminding yourself of inspirational stories such as this will help you experience the benefits of gratitude, even if the story doesn't directly relate to you. If it moves you emotionally and fills you with hope, inspiration and appreciation for humanity, it can uplift you and encourages you to go out and help others, too. No doubt you are constantly bombarded with daily negative news in the media, in your workplace and in society more generally, so when you do hear positive stories of compassion, kindness and helpfulness, you are likely to experience internal joy.

## Self-reflection

1. Can you remember a time when you received genuine thanks and gratitude from someone? What did you do and how was this acknowledged? Most importantly, how did this gratitude make you feel?

2. If you can't remember a time you received gratitude, do you have a particular story that comes to mind of someone receiving help in a moment of need, and the receiver of the help being hugely grateful to the person who helped them?

3. What thoughts and feelings came up for you when you read the story of Derek and his father? Did it fill you with love and admiration for a father and son's relationship, and for the courage and determination of Derek to complete the race, pushing far beyond both his physical and emotional pain? Are you thinking about how you would have responded in that situation if you were either Derek or Jim? Or perhaps you are thinking about their father-son relationship — is it something you've always longed for or have not had the opportunity to experience yet? Take some time to process your thoughts, and really think about how this story, and ones similar to it, make you feel.

# Reframing experiences via a gratitude lens

As I mention in chapter 3, the human brain is a meaning-making machine. In fact, it dislikes ambiguity or feelings of conflict and actively seeks to create meaning from all the experiences, interactions and feelings you encounter. This is fabulous because it means you can control the meaning your brain attaches to situations and interactions you experience. That's right—you can constructively change the narrative and meaning you attach to a particular event. In this way, by adopting a gratitude mindset, you can even look at setbacks and adversity via a lens of self-learning and growth. With compassion toward yourself and your situation, you can identify learnings and be grateful for your situation, even if it's far from ideal, because it's likely to provide you with the opportunity to grow, learn and evolve. Perhaps you'll even have a chance to reinvent yourself, revise your purpose and provide greater clarity on what's important to you.

Back when my husband and I were navigating through a rough patch in our marriage, Friday evenings became synonymous with petty arguments and tension. It felt like we were constantly at odds with each other, grappling with our own personal struggles and failing to connect with each other. I can't even recall the specifics of one particular argument; all I remember is the stifling heat of the moment as we bickered in the living room while our 18-month-old son was playing with his toys nearby.

Something completely remarkable then happened. Our little boy, playing with his toys in the chaos of our squabbling, decided to take matters into his own hands. He fetched his tiny wooden stool and positioned himself before the cluttered bookshelf in our lounge. Among the vast collection of different books, framed family photographs and toy boxes, his small finger pointed with determination to one book, and he reached out to grab it to show us. It wasn't any book. The book he picked out was *The Happiness Trap* by psychologist Dr Russ Harris, with its cover of a big yellow smiley face. He looked at us both with his innocent eyes. My husband and I froze in disbelief, staring at each other and then at our son.

It was like a slap in the face but in the softest, most profound way possible. There we were, tangled up in our own mess, while this tiny, amazing human reminded us of what truly mattered. At that very moment, a wave of realisation and shame washed over us—what were we doing to ourselves and to our little family, and how could we let our problems spill over like this, especially in front of our little son?

Among all these feelings, was a deep sense of gratitude because it felt like the universe was giving us a gentle nudge, urging us to pay attention to the bigger picture. We scooped our son up in our arms, hugged him tightly and made a solemn commitment to each other. From that day forward, we vowed never to let our disagreements shake our family dynamic again. Instead, we pledged to work together to strengthen our bond and navigate our challenges as a united front.

That evening remains etched in our memories as a poignant reminder of our journey—the highs, the lows and everything in between. To this day, we are deeply grateful for the lessons we uncovered from that transformative moment, which ultimately paved the way for deeper understanding, mutual respect and a stronger, more resilient marriage. As a beautiful testament to our growth, our son eventually welcomed a cheeky, feisty and spirited little brother into our family two years later.

This is the true power of gratitude—because it is a gift that has the power to keep giving. Over time, as you intentionally and regularly practise gratitude in the way detailed in the following section, you will start to rewire your neural pathways and, through the process of neuroplasticity, transform your brain to surpass its automatic negativity bias. With greater ease and intentionality, you will be able to focus on gratitude even when your life is chaotic, uncertain and trying. This part of the 5Qs Formula will transform your mindset into one that is more optimistic, appreciative and seeking fulfilment. This will help you maximise your productivity impact and your experience of daily joy.

# Applying the 5Qs Formula: Question two

Question two of the 5Qs Formula comprises two parts and taps into the essential aspect of gratitude. Answering both parts will only take one to two minutes, once you have done the pre-thinking and have started to build your momentum of applying the 5Qs Formula daily. By hacking into your brain to release greater levels of dopamine and serotonin, you will feel more positive, confident, capable and resilient to go about achieving your day's activities with joy, feeling fulfilled and satisfied. In this way, you will set yourself to be effective and energised throughout your day. Let's start with part A.

## Applying question two, part A

What experiences, things or people in your life are you grateful for because they inspire you to be a better version of yourself?

The crux of part A lies in its ability to 'inspire you to be a better version of yourself'. This concept is pivotal in leading a purposeful, impactful and fulfilled life, because it encourages continuous growth and improvement. Coined by basketball coach Pat Riley, the idea of striving to be 1 per cent better each day serves as a driving force behind personal and professional development. It's the catalyst that can propel you toward becoming a better human, leader, manager, employee, business owner, parent, sibling, professional, athlete or student.

Central to this question is recognising and appreciating unique experiences, individuals, situations and objects in your life that contribute to your growth. These are the sources of inspiration that compel you to live in alignment with your values and strive for excellence.

To achieve the goal of being 1 per cent better each day, it's essential to acknowledge and identify these sources of inspiration consciously. Whether it's a supportive mentor, a challenging yet rewarding experience, or a cherished possession, these elements serve as reminders of the journey toward self-improvement and fulfilment. Embracing gratitude and appreciation for these influences fosters a mindset of continuous growth and empowers you to embody the best version of yourself.

Take Hayley, an accountant who has worked for a professional accountancy firm for the last eight years. It's a busy organisation, with consistent cycles of heavy workload, tight client deadlines and high stress levels. Recently, a new manager has put her under constant pressure to meet expectations. The organisation has not been performing well financially and some roles are at risk—understandably, the job insecurity fills Hayley with anxiety and uncertainty. She rarely receives praise or recognition from her manager and, therefore, feels undervalued and unappreciated, and has developed feelings of resentment toward her employer. She often works long hours, including evenings and several weekends a month, which is unpaid overtime. Work dominates her time and energy, making it harder for her to appreciate other aspects of her life. She also fears not having the time to be able to care for her ageing parents in the coming years. Lately, she has found herself becoming reactive to others and feeling disengaged, and searching for some transparent communication from her manager about any potential redundancy package. In any spare time, she has started looking for roles elsewhere. Significant criteria in deciding her next role is knowing the type of manager she will report to and working in a supportive and positive workplace culture, which promotes a healthy work–life balance. She knew currently she could not separate her role from her self-identity.

When Hayley spent time responding to part A of question two of the 5Qs Formula, it helped her remember previous mentors who had built successful careers and somehow managed to fulfil other responsibilities in their lives also. It made her realise that she too could be clearer on her boundaries, and that she could be grateful for being able to take her time to find a role that aligns to the type of workplace culture she wants to work in. She realised she was also grateful for what she had learnt about leadership from her current manager, with the experience making it more explicit what good leadership was and wasn't and what type of leader she wanted to become. She was also grateful for the barista at her local coffee shop in the mornings, who would always ask her how she was. It reminded her of the importance of checking in with people and seeing how they are, and not assuming most people are always okay.

Another example is Matthew, a working professional with three young children—a 13-year-old daughter, a six-year-old son and an eight-month-old baby daughter. He often finds himself feeling tired, overwhelmed and in a form of 'survival mode' as he and his partner juggle the volume of tasks each week. These tasks include handling multiple responsibilities, childcare, work commitments and deliverables, household chores, children's activities, school events and sports, as well as his and his partner's personal commitments.

These responsibilities constantly demand his time and energy and, unfortunately, he feels often overwhelmed with no time to focus on gratitude.

He found himself slipping into the cycle of directly or inadvertently comparing his parenting style with others, and even at times comparing his children to others. He was holding himself to unrealistic standards, which often left him feeling inadequate, dissatisfied and miserable. Not to forget, he was also dealing with all the different age-related challenges his children were facing.

Parenthood is undeniably a journey filled with moments of immense happiness, love and joy. However, it's essential to acknowledge that along with these positive experiences come challenges that require careful consideration. In Matthew's case, these challenges ranged from the sleepless nights with his newborn and navigating the emotional tantrums of his six year old, to dealing with the hormonal changes, complexities of relationships and rebellious attitude of his 13 year old. All of these challenges, alongside his work challenges, made not dwelling on his struggles difficult for Matthew. With such busyness, worry and parent guilt, Matthew found it hard to prioritise gratitude.

He looked at ways to create space and time to implement the 5Qs Formula before the kids woke up in the morning, and decided to allocate himself five minutes to go through the questions as he had his morning coffee. If this didn't happen, he would take five minutes after school drop-off, once he had parked his car at his workplace and before he went into the office.

Finding this time to implement the 5Qs Formula, and answering question two in particular, helped Matthew be more present at work and with his children. It strengthened his relationship with his children and helped him focus on what he, his partner and his children were doing well as a family. Focusing on gratitude helped him to realise how much his children had helped him become much more fun and expressive. He also noticed that he had become more planned and organised, which meant he had more time to do all the things his responsibilities required of him.

Remember—each day presents an opportunity to cultivate a mindset infused with inspiration and growth. This question helps you nurture gratitude not just for the positives in life, but also for the lessons learned from challenges and even from those who may have caused you pain. Consider the teachers, mentors or coaches who invested in your development, as well as the adversities that shaped your understanding of how you wish to interact with others. Even negative experiences can catalyse personal growth, fostering clarity about your values and guiding principles. This insight and reflection can help you become clear on what behaviours inspire you and which don't.

You're often drawn to individuals who possess qualities you admire or wish to cultivate within yourself. You are even more likely to find inspiration in those who reflect aspects of your own character that you haven't fully acknowledged or expressed as yet. Psychologists call this phenomenon 'perception is projection', where your views of others are heavily influenced by your internal thoughts, motivations and psychological make-up. Reflecting on those who inspire you often triggers the release of positive chemicals in your brain. It instils hope and motivation within you by signalling that if they can achieve their goals, so can you. These examples inspire by giving you hope that you have some of the qualities you admire in a particular person—you just need to discover and unlock them within yourself. Additionally, reflecting on those who inspire you reinforces your sense of self-worth, making you feel good about yourself too.

Contemplating why specific experiences or people have inspired you deepens the benefits of this gratitude practice. This first part of question two helps you delve into the qualities or actions that make those experiences or people significant to you and your growth. This process strengthens your connection to those sources of gratitude and helps you better understand your values, priorities and relationships.

Your responses here could simply be a list of the people or experiences that have inspired you to be a better version of yourself. Importantly, though, make sure you note what in particular inspired you. You don't need to write much in your journal here, just one or two specific bullet points. For example:

*'A new client inspired me to be vulnerable when I am finding things overwhelming; in this way, I can ask for the relevant support or help I need.'*

*'My boss has taken the time to understand my career goals and believes in me to achieve them. I really appreciate the support they are providing, including constructive feedback and praise.'*

*'My uncle inspired me to be compassionate and empathetic towards others, as I witnessed him consistently helping those in need without expecting anything in return.'*

*'A close friend of mine inspired me to prioritise self-care and mental wellbeing by openly sharing their journey of overcoming burnout and implementing healthy habits into their daily routine.'*

*'I've been inspired by a business owner's commitment to ethical practices and corporate social responsibility. Their dedication to giving back to the community and minimising environmental impact has motivated me to integrate similar principles into my own business decisions.'*

*'I've been inspired by a classmate who consistently demonstrates a strong work ethic and resilience. Their determination to overcome obstacles and strive for academic excellence has encouraged me to adopt a similar mindset and approach to my studies.'*

You might find yourself consistently inspired by the same example each day or, if you interact with various people throughout your week, you may discover new sources of inspiration regularly. Whether it's a recurring influence or a fresh encounter, make sure you take a moment to reflect on what inspires you and jot down your thoughts.

You may also find inspiration from characters in books, TV shows or movies. Additionally, if you enjoy exploring new places or trying out new experiences, take a moment to reflect on those encounters too, and jot down a few sentences or bullet points to capture the essence of what inspired you about each interaction or experience.

For example, you may have been inspired by a place you visited, as was my client Prem:

*During a trip to Kyoto, Japan, I was deeply inspired by the serene temples and traditional tea houses, with the harmonious blend of nature and craftsmanship. This experience encouraged me to embrace mindfulness and simplicity in my daily life.*

Feel free to vary your responses each time you reflect on this question.

## Applying question two, part B

Think of a time you have received gratitude and appreciation from someone; how did it make you feel?

This question prompts you to recall a time when you received genuine thanks from someone. Reflect on the individual who expressed gratitude, how they conveyed it, and its impact on you. If you can't recall a personal experience, keep in mind that you can also consider a story you've heard or read about someone else receiving gratitude (similar to the example shared earlier in this chapter about Derek Redmond). Capture the essence of the gratitude and its effects on you in two or three brief bullet points.

For example:

- 'My co-worker thanked me for staying late to help them with a project, expressing genuine appreciation for my support.'

- 'Their sincere gratitude made me feel valued and motivated to continue offering assistance whenever I can and when it's needed.'

Or:

- 'A friend sent me a heartfelt note expressing gratitude for always being there to listen and offer support during a difficult time in their life.'

- 'Their words of thanks filled me with warmth and reaffirmed the importance of being there for others in times of need.'

Remembering times when you have received genuine gratitude from others triggers your brain to also remember the rewarding aspects of the experience, which gives you the dopamine hit and motivates you to do your best in all you do. It makes you feel appreciated, acknowledged, seen, heard and valued. All of these factors increase your mood, energy and outlook. As your cup fills, you feel satisfied and fulfilled. This influences your interactions with others as you are likely to radiate more positive energy, optimism and a keenness to help others. Humans like to help humans! We have a natural inclination to assist others.

Once you do the 5Qs Formula daily, you will notice key themes in the things or people who inspire you, and when others have expressed gratitude to you. Knowing the key themes does not mean you should stop practising both parts of this question, because the actual practice of gratitude in question two will help you continue to impact your mood, attitude and motivation levels.

# Summary

From a young age, we are taught to be grateful for what we have, those who help us and the opportunities we get to experience. I remember being younger and thinking that if I weren't grateful, the experiences, relationships or things that I enjoyed would be gone. For me, practising gratitude became a practice based on fear—fearing losing something I enjoyed or valued—rather than a practice based on an abundance mindset.

The more you are grateful, the more you get to be grateful for. This shift in my thinking really started to happen when I studied the psychological science behind practising regular gratitude, and how this changes brain chemistry, impacting mood, attention and outlook.

Focusing your attention on gratitude and being thankful by acknowledging specific blessings in your life instantly provides you with an emotional and psychological uplift; it paves the way for abundance and releases serotonin, a hormone that stabilises your mood and wellbeing. Research shows that it only takes two minutes of gratitude to change your brain chemistry enough to have a positive, measurable effect on your entire day.

It's easy to start your day without pausing to think about gratitude in the way prescribed by question two of the 5Qs Formula, especially if most of your days start off in the same way and are full of 'ordinary moments'. As Brené Brown shares, we often get caught up in chasing the extraordinary moments, yet it's the most 'ordinary' moments we miss the most—for example, the sunrise each morning, sleeping peacefully in your comfortable sanctuary and having access to various foods and clothing at your disposal. We often take the things and people in front of us for granted and can quite easily go through our day without expressing gratitude for all our fortunes. So do remember to recall those who inspire you to be a better version of yourself and those who express their thanks to you, and ensure you express gratitude for all your fortunes and gifts in your day too. As bestselling author Shauna Niequist recommends, 'When life is sweet, say thank you and celebrate. When life is bitter, say thank you and grow.'

# Key takeaways

- Gratitude requires intentional and deliberate practice; it's not something that comes naturally to most humans.

- Recognising what could get in the way of you expressing or receiving gratitude is essential. Once you are aware, you can do something about it to help you reap the benefits of practising gratitude.

- The benefits of practising gratitude include psychological, physical, social and spiritual wellbeing improvements.

- Key neurotransmitters involved in gratitude are dopamine and serotonin.

- Gratitude improves social connection, empathy, resiliency, optimism, motivation, sleep, immunity and overall wellbeing.

- Expressing and receiving gratitude cannot be faked; it must always be real, sincere and genuine.

- Practising two minutes of gratitude each morning (as per question two of the 5Qs Formula) will rewire your neural pathways and cultivate a mindset of appreciation and optimism, leading to greater levels of self-confidence and resilience, which helps you to maximise your daily productivity and joy.

# CHAPTER 5

# Cultivating positivity and personal growth

*Question three: What is working well for you right now, and what could be working better for you?*

Without intentionally priming your brain at the start of the day to focus on the positive and consider potential threats, it is likely to be governed by the negativity bias, reducing your productivity, optimal functioning and joy.

This third question of the 5Qs Formula helps you hack your brain's negativity bias daily in an effective and time-efficient way. You will be able achieve what you want every day from a doing and feeling perspective, and feel energised and joyful.

# The strength of your negativity bias

As shared in the previous chapter, the human brain is hardwired to detect negatives, because it has evolved to detect potential hazards, threats and risks to ensure your survival. While the brain does this from a survival instinct, the negativity bias influences what you focus your attention on. This, in turn, impacts your mood and subjective wellbeing, and your interpretation of your own satisfaction, happiness and fulfilment in life.

For example, you are likely to remember when someone in your team let you down by not doing what they said they were going to do, when a project went over budget, when you received a customer complaint, when your child misbehaved or had difficulties at school, when you received poor grades on an exam or assignments, or when you felt frustrated because your partner or children only completed some of the house chores and not everything you mutually had agreed on. Your brain will tend to recall, dwell on and seek out negative events or interpretations of situations, often overlooking or downplaying the positive ones.

This tendency means you will need to put in more brain energy and effort to remember all the other times your team completed a task you asked for on time. Or the times projects have been delivered within or to budget, or when you have received incredible positive customer feedback. Or the times your child has listened and behaved well or when you did well in an academic achievement, had an enjoyable and successful learning experience or acknowledged the completed house chores.

The brain's tendency to focus on the negative can make it seem like positive events, interactions and circumstances are less frequent or less significant than they actually are. This skewed perception occurs because negative experiences leave a stronger impression on the brain, often overshadowing the positive ones. Your brain's primary concern is to keep you safe, so it gives more weight to negative experiences, feedback or events to prevent them from recurring and harming you. As a result, it's important to remember that your view of situations, experiences or interactions may be unfairly coloured or distorted by this negativity bias.

## Five ways your brain can deceive you

While your brain has evolved in magnificent ways to help you learn, grow and thrive, you must still be cautious about believing everything it tells you. The brain deploys hacks and short cuts to make sense of all the information it receives and pays attention to, conserving energy to focus on what it needs to in order to keep you safe. This includes keeping you safe from physical hazards such as oncoming traffic, slippery floors and falling objects, as well as psychological hazards such as interpersonal conflicts, harassment, embarrassment or even environmental hazards such as poor lighting, loud noises and extreme temperatures. The world can be a dangerous place!

When you are tired, overloaded, under pressure, or feel threatened or out of your comfort zone, your brain will deploy a short cut (referred to as 'cognitive errors' or 'heuristics' by psychologists) to help you act quickly, because it believes you are in danger. However, these short cuts often distort your thinking and judgements, leading to misinterpretations or misguided reactions to situations, individuals or events. Such distortions can unfairly affect your focus, attention, mood and motivation for the upcoming day—and potentially distract your attention, dampening your spirits and making things feel harder to accomplish.

Understanding how your brain functions, particularly in stressful or overwhelming situations, is crucial for maximising your productivity. You can strive to maintain a balanced mindset and approach by recognising both beneficial and detrimental cognitive patterns. This recognition and insight will help you to make rational and thoughtful decisions, and enable you to act calmly rather than impulsively or reactively.

Your brain can deceive you of the truth in five common ways.

## 'All or nothing' thinking

This is where you see things as extremes or binary—as either 'everything is great', or 'it's a total disaster'. So you either aced that presentation, for example, or you made a total mess of it. Instead of acknowledging the nuances, such as the areas where you did well and where you could improve, you're stuck in this extreme thinking.

We know life is far too complex for situations or events to be broken into these two extremes and that, instead, so many shades of grey exist in between. This is why the third question of the 5Qs Formula prompts you to recognise what is working well for you each day and what could be working better for you. Unpacking and discovering what lies within the shades of grey is important, because this is where more accurate meaning and interpretation can be realised. You can use insights gained to effectively motivate and channel your attention to achieve what you need to do on a particular day.

## Mental filter

Due to the negative bias already mentioned earlier, you can have a mental filter that means you only recall negative outcomes, events or interactions that happened to you during your day and dismiss anything positive. For example, you had a productive day at work, but one minor criticism from your boss sticks with you, overshadowing all your other accomplishments that day. You filter out the positives and dwell solely on the one piece of negative feedback.

It can be easy to fall prey to this trap when you feel downtrodden and things feel challenging. Your brain will likely forget all the great things you have achieved so far, and particularly how you felt when you achieved or did something different, because it does not assess these as being an immediate threat to you. Therefore, your brain is not motivated to remember or recall them readily. Again, the third question of the 5Qs Formula prompts you to remember these positives, giving you a more balanced and supportive perspective to help you achieve your goals.

## 'Should' statements

'Should' statements occur when you attempt to motivate yourself by dwelling on what you think you 'should' be able to achieve — and then you judge yourself critically and often unfairly when you don't. For example, 'I should have reached a certain level in my career by now', 'I should be exercising seven days a week' or 'I should have completed my assignment by now'. Or you think, *I should be cooking gourmet meals every night*, even though you have a busy schedule and often resort to quick 15-minute dinners. This self-imposed pressure to meet unrealistic standards leads to feelings of guilt and inadequacy.

By allowing this 'should' language of thought to happen repeatedly, you can severely limit, disempower and judge yourself harshly. Be mindful of when 'should' thinking comes into your mind, because it is often derived from beliefs you've held about yourself for a long time or the ideals and views of others, which may not be relevant or essential to you in your life right now.

## Mind reading

This deception happens when you make quick assumptions and conclude that someone is being negative toward you, without any demonstrable evidence and without taking into account other possible explanations. For example, say you send a message to a friend and they don't respond immediately, but you feel confident they have read your message. Instead of considering that your friend might be busy or away from their phone, you assume they're deliberately ignoring you and feel hurt, disappointed, let down and potentially rejected. Taking a moment to integrate these assumptions can help you come up with alternative and reasonably plausible ways of making sense of a situation.

## Over-generalisation

Over-generalisation happens when you face one challenge or negative outcome, and then become convinced this will be repeated in all future similar situations. For example, 'I had a super unproductive day; the rest of the week or month will be like this'. Or you have a disagreement with a co-worker and now believe all future interactions with them will be unpleasant. You generalise one negative experience to all similar situations, assuming they will all turn out the same way. Of course, this over-generalised way of thinking is unhelpful, because every day presents unique opportunities and challenges and does not need to be like the day before. Similarly, every interaction is unique and does not need to define a relationship. Focusing on each day and each interaction in its wholeness and uniqueness allows specificity and relevance to occur, which is far more meaningful and helpful to you than over-generalising.

Being super mindful of how your brain can deceive you in these five typical ways is extremely powerful. Having insight into these deceptions can prevent you from falling into these mind traps, which will influence how you think, feel and act. Learning to recognise these mind traps in your own thinking can help you move forward quickly to get the best out of yourself each day.

## Constructive reframing to help overcome your brain's bias

When you fall prey to one of the five deceptions, reframing and changing how you look at things will help. Psychologists call this 'cognitive reframing', and it involves actively altering your perspective or interpretation of a situation, event, interaction or thought to see it in a more positive and balanced light.

Three quick steps to move out of unhelpful ways of thinking are:

1.  Ask yourself regularly, 'Could I be letting any of the five deceptions cloud my thinking about a particular situation, interaction, event or circumstance?'

2.  If you notice you are, ask yourself, 'What alternative ways of looking at this situation, interaction, event or circumstance are possible?' or 'What are the facts of the situation I am aware of?' and 'What assumptions am I making?'

3.  Finally, ask yourself, 'What is the most helpful way I can think about the situation to help me reach a more balanced view and understanding of it?'

Unexpected or unforeseen challenges may disrupt your plans or throw off your morning routine as you start your day. For instance, you might oversleep after hitting the snooze button on your alarm clock. Instead of letting frustration take over and giving up, you can reassess your priorities, adjust your schedule, and see what other support or resources you can lean on. You can always maintain momentum and achieve productivity despite such challenges by staying flexible, proactive and open to change. (And to avoid snoozing my alarm clock in the first place, I often remind myself of this phrase, 'If you snooze, you lose'. Not wanting to attach myself to an identity of losing drives me out of bed.)

Say you are a business owner and you find yourself facing a drop in sales. Instead of panicking and assuming failure, you can assess the market trends, seek customer feedback and explore different marketing strategies. In this way, you are focusing on proactive solutions rather than dwelling on negative interpretations and remaining stuck. By being open to new ways and taking positive actions you can steer your business toward success.

Or imagine you are a leader or manager, and your project faces unexpected delays. Understandably, this makes you feel frustrated and perhaps you start to doubt yourself. Instead of fixating and being stuck on the perceived failure, you can ask yourself if you are falling into one of the five deception thinking traps. You may realise you are falling into 'all or nothing' thinking, assuming the one setback means the project has failed. This thinking is not going to serve you well. Here is an opportunity to consider alternative viewpoints and start problem-solving rather than ruminating on the negative outcomes. Reframing your thinking about the situation will help you to approach the situation with a clearer, more balanced mindset. Others around you will also likely be inspired by your effective leadership and problem-solving capabilities. In this way, you make an even bigger positive difference as you role-model adaptability and resiliency.

Another example is if you are a student and you receive a lower grade on an assignment than hoped for. Instead of immediately assuming failure and feeling discouraged, you can reflect on the feedback provided by your lecturer and identify areas for improvement. From this reflection, you may spend more time studying, change the structure of your response to the next assignment, or clarify what other information your assignment needs to include. This reflection and reframing will help you work out your next steps to help you do better in your next assignment.

I refer to this skill as 'learning agility', whereby you seek to continuously redirect your focus and attention to make things better, focusing on what is in your control, and proactively taking steps to move forward rather than letting yourself become stuck. Again, not all is lost; only learning and growth can be gained.

# The paradox of perfection

No-one has a perfect life or even a perfect day; by that, I mean not everything for anyone is ever wholly ideal or without its challenges. While it may look like someone's life or day is ideal from the outside, everyone faces their own set of difficulties, imperfections, obstacles and circumstances. This highlights the unique and individualised complexity and diversity of human experiences. Pursuing and striving for perfection can ironically make you feel stuck, inflexible and unhappy. Therefore, pursuing perfection hinders rather than helps your productivity joy.

Research shows that humans tend to perceive others' lives as more perfect or idealised than their own, a phenomenon psychologists call 'social comparison bias'. This bias occurs because most people tend to portray their lives in a more positive light to others, creating an illusion of perfection or idealism. Individuals do this to:

- manage the impressions others have of them

- gain approval or validation from others

- feel better about themselves (because it helps them maintain a positive self-image)

- increase their social desirability.

This portrayal typically involves showcasing positive aspects of your life while downplaying or concealing less desirable or negative elements you don't want others to know or see. You don't need to go very far to experience social comparison—you have the means in the palm of your hand. When you scroll through social media on your phone, including Instagram, LinkedIn and Facebook, you will see images, stories and updates on all the 'amazing' things people are experiencing, doing or achieving in their lives. Remember, again, most people only post and share the most positive or 'glorified' aspects of their lives, so you are not seeing the whole picture of their lives.

## Self-reflection

How does comparing yourself to others really make you feel? Do you feel empowered and motivated to attain similar perceived success or fulfilment levels? Or does it leave you feeling inadequate, not good enough, not doing well enough, and ultimately dissatisfied with aspects of your own life?

While for some people, the comparison inspires them to achieve more for themselves, for most people it's the opposite, and this tends not to serve them well. It's helpful to know how you respond to social comparison—whether it uplifts you or not, and whether it impacts how you feel about yourself and what you need or want to achieve. In this way, you will become clearer on what drives your choices and behaviours concerning how you spend time and energy each day. (For more on knowing your values and drivers, see chapter 7.)

## Limiting the distraction of social comparison

A helpful tip for staying focused on your day and life is to limit your social media consumption. By allocating specific time to scrolling or social media consumption, you establish boundaries on your social media usage and prevent the all-too-common distractions of the social comparison bias and lost productivity that come from frequently checking your phone.

As well as the negative feelings stemming from social comparison, this loss of productivity is related to the time spent switching cognitive/mental focus. Many executives, busy professionals and students believe multitasking is essential to managing their busy schedules, but it actually hurts productivity. A momentary shift and switch in attention from one task to another, such as checking emails, taking a phone call or checking your LinkedIn notifications, can increase the time needed to complete your main task by up to 25 per cent, due to a phenomenon known as 'switching time'.

Your brain can only focus intensely on one thing at a time, so multitasking or quickly switching from one task to another does not optimise your brain's functioning to help you be the most productive you. Concentrating fully for 60 to 90 minutes at a time is far more conducive to your attention and focus, followed by a quality break (anywhere from 15 to 30 minutes) before focusing on a new task. Similarly, turning off notifications makes you less likely to be tempted to check your devices and be less distracted during times of focused work.

Putting your phone in a different room or away from your workstation can help you to focus and concentrate for bursts of focused time. Your brain naturally has a limited capacity for sustained attention, and it is easily drawn to things within your immediate environment—that is, in sight, in mind versus out of sight and out of mind. Removing distractions such as your phone or turning off notifications will create a focused environment for deep concentration. This will allow you to enjoy dedicated bursts of uninterrupted time on your tasks, and you will be less tempted to switch between tasks or lose focus. This will help you work more effectively for longer periods of time without distraction, leading to greater productivity and satisfaction.

## *The power of priming*

Asking yourself 'What is working well today?' at the start of the day is priming your brain to look within and around you, in your environment, to identify things you perceive to be positive, helpful and conducive to your day. This question is designed to prime your brain intentionally. As mentioned, focusing on what works well for you will not happen automatically due to the brain's negativity bias.

If you do no intentional priming, even without realising it your brain will focus on detecting things around you that it perceives to be not working well, not ideal or perfect, or not suitable for you. The things it detects as not working well or not ideal are based on your expectations, ideals, previous experiences or comparative norms. As an example of this, we recently moved into our new home, and I've found it difficult not to focus on the renovations that need doing, despite knowing that we plan to tackle these later in the year.

Indeed, most people's natural inclination is to view things through a pessimistic lens, focusing on what's wrong rather than acknowledging even the smallest positive aspects of your day or week. However, by actively seeking out and recognising small victories, no matter how insignificant they may seem, you gradually accumulate a reserve of positive acknowledgements. These moments of acknowledgement serve as internal credits, boosting your optimism and energy levels. This shift from a pessimistic to an optimistic mindset fosters feelings of encouragement, hope and overall positivity, helping you to see the brighter side of situations—that 'things are not so bad, after all!'—and helping you to feel a sense of overall contentment.

Some may argue this is simply looking at things from a cup-half-full (rather than half-empty) perspective. I would partially agree. However, this approach is not about being disillusioned and kidding yourself that 'everything' is fine when you know it's not or when you know things could be better.

You're not hoping to convince yourself that everything is positive and perfect when it's not and can't possibly be. Your brain and body need genuine reassurance that things are okay, not just verbal affirmations. Simply saying 'everything is fine' when you're fully aware that it is not creates a disconnect within your mind, and this is when your brain will focus even more on the negatives to try to make sense of the disconnect. Therefore, it's important to address the actual issues you're facing rather than trying to force yourself into a state of false positivity. You can't trick or lie to your body or mind—it will only feel the disconnect as conflict. Acknowledging and addressing challenges realistically allows you to work towards genuine solutions and maintain a healthier mental and emotional balance.

Importantly, this is where the second part of question three in the 5Qs Formula—which I cover in more detail later in this chapter—becomes vital. This second part asks you to consider what could be working better for you. Responding fully to question three and considering both aspects (what is working well and what could be working better) means you can reap the full benefits of this intentional priming hack.

For now, let's keep focusing on part one of question three. Once you start to notice things that are going well, you will start to notice and spot even more things in your environment or within you that help you move forward with your goals for the day. This shift happens because your brain is primed to direct its attention toward finding relevant cues, and de-selecting irrelevant cues. You're more prepared to observe and embrace possibilities that support your goals actively.

Here is an example of priming your brain you may relate to if, like me, you're constantly misplacing your keys in your home and searching for them. When searching for the keys, your brain is primed to look for the specific object. As you scan your home, your brain becomes more attentive to spot objects resembling keys, such as metallic shapes, familiar colours and keychain designs. Because your brain is primed to look for the keys, it actively filters out irrelevant information to focus on similar objects. This heightened attention to specific and relevant details increases the likelihood of spotting your keys in your home, among all the other objects. When you prime your brain to look for something, it will work hard by selecting its attention to find what you have primed it to look for, and it will de-select paying attention to anything irrelevant and unimportant to the specific activity.

This is why asking your brain to identify 'what is working well for you today' is a powerful way to channel your attention and focus on identifying the positive aspects in your environment, in how you feel, or in things that have happened or are going to happen. Identifying the positive aspects and those that you believe will serve you well enables you to experience positive emotions, which release 'feel good' neurotransmitters such as serotonin, making you feel good, motivated and inspired for your day.

Remember — the key to responding to this question is acknowledging the small recent victories, achievements, moments or aspects of joy or positivity in the last 24 hours. Your brain is likely to remember the most recent things or experiences that occurred as they will still be present in your short-term memory, making it quicker and easier for you to recall and reap the benefits of their positive associated emotions. Psychologists refer to this as the 'recency effect'. Later in this chapter, in the section 'Applying the 5Qs Formula: Question 3', I provide a few examples from some of my clients' responses to this question.

# The link between optimism and resiliency

Having a positive mood increases your levels of hopefulness and optimism. Optimism is an attribute of hope, a belief that things will work out for the best. Optimists believe that good things are possible even when negative or bad things occur. They choose a positive outlook, viewing challenges as temporary and manageable and setbacks as opportunities for growth and learning. Those with a pessimistic outlook, on the other hand, tend to see negative events or circumstances as permanent, pervasive and uncontrollable. Let's be clear: optimism is not about wishful thinking or denying reality. However, it does involve a mindset that actively seeks and focuses on the potential for positive outcomes, even in the most challenging situations.

## Self-reflection

1. Would you say you are primarily an optimist or a pessimist?

2. What would those closest to you describe you as? Do you think people in different aspects of your life would have different views about whether they perceive you as an optimist or a pessimist?

Dr Martin Seligman, the father of positive psychology, undertook over 15 years of research into what makes people resilient. He concluded that part of the answer is optimism, as well as other factors such as social support, problem-solving skills, adaptability and finding meaning in adversity. In his book *Learned Optimism*, Seligman shares that optimism can be learned and developed, at any stage of life. And the benefits of doing so are clear. His research shows that those who adopt an optimistic mindset are better equipped to cope with stress and setbacks. Because they are likely to maintain a positive outlook, they will bounce back from their setbacks quicker than someone with a pessimistic outlook. Optimism also provides a buffer against the negative effects of stress when you experience challenging situations, hardships and pressures, such as juggling multiple commitments, demanding roles, intense deadlines, or even trauma and grief.

Remember—everyone can learn optimism at any stage of life. And question three of the 5Qs Formula helps you develop an optimistically balanced mindset. With daily practice, you can cultivate a strong level of optimism within you, which will become a vital tool in helping you experience daily productivity and joy.

The link between optimism and resiliency is very much relevant to your daily life, because each day your personal and professional life will present its own challenges, uncertainties and opportunities. Resilient and optimistic individuals approach challenges with a sense of resourcefulness and creativity. This empowers them to take control of their circumstances and they believe in themselves and that they will find a way through.

This is the opposite of those who experience 'learned helplessness'. Studies, beginning with research on dogs and subsequently extending to humans, have shown that individuals who perceive limited control over their circumstances tend to cease seeking alternatives and remain stuck and trapped in their own way. This also leads to lowered levels of self-confidence and a reduced belief in their capacity to enact change. When people feel they have little or no control over their circumstances, they are more prone to experience mental health issues such as depression, anxiety and chronic stress, because they feel helpless and disempowered.

I remember coaching a senior director at a prominent professional services firm who experienced a significant blow to her confidence, self-worth and overall psychological wellbeing when her role was made redundant. Having been with the company for several years, she felt that if the organisation truly valued her, they would have either found another position for her or fought to retain her role. Following her departure from the organisation, she withdrew from others for months, retreating into herself and coping with feelings of hurt and disappointment through binge eating and nightly wine consumption. She could not even contemplate seeking new opportunities and advancing her career. Through the personalised coaching, we prioritised her wellbeing, worked on rebuilding her self-confidence and helped her gain clarity regarding her identity, strengths and impact. Gradually, she began to feel prepared to explore new career prospects and, with time, her overall wellbeing, self-confidence and self-esteem transformed. She learnt how to change her internal narrative into one that served her well to take steps forward into a more brighter and connected future. She learned how to become unstuck and get out of her own way.

Setbacks like this can get the best of us, even if you are generally optimistic and try to hold a positive and balanced outlook. Surrounding yourself with a supportive network of individuals who know your capabilities and are willing to stand by you and constructively support you (not pander to you) during tough times can be immensely beneficial to your path to becoming unstuck.

Seeking guidance from a trusted advisor such as a psychology coach can also provide you with invaluable tools and strategies to help you navigate through setbacks and recharge your resilience.

It's crucial to recognise that resilience is not innate or fixed; you are not born with a 'fixed level of resilience'. In fact, resilience is a skill that can be developed through your lived experience of getting through challenges and setbacks. As you continue to face and overcome challenges, you build your resilience levels and you will notice your personal growth unfold. Over time, obstacles that once seemed insurmountable gradually lose their power to derail you.

For example, imagine you struggled with public speaking and could only do this by taking a beta blocker to manage your anxiety in advance. With practice, determination and specialist psychology coaching support, you gradually become more confident and skilled, to the point where you actually now don't mind presenting. You now have the confidence to do it without taking a beta blocker, and you also receive praise from others when they hear you speak. Remember—each and every setback becomes a stepping stone toward you becoming stronger, more capable and more resilient than before.

## Self-reflection

1.  Recall a moment when you faced a significant challenge or setback, one that deeply affected you, shook your confidence, or made you question your beliefs or values.

2.  Now, reflect on the specific support that helped you navigate through this tough period. Consider whether it was something someone said to you, a piece of advice or encouragement, a book,

an article you read or a podcast you listened to, a particular activity or practice you engaged in, or any other form of support that played a crucial role in helping you cope and overcome the adversity.

By engaging in this brief self-reflection exercise, you gain powerful insight into the types of support that are most effective for you during challenging times. By examining past experiences of adversity and the support that helped you overcome them, you can identify patterns and strategies that have proven beneficial for your wellbeing and resilience. This self-awareness will give you the strength to proactively seek out similar or even different forms of support in the future, as well as cultivate a deeper understanding of your own coping mechanisms and needs. This also helps you embrace the reality that your life, like everyone else's, will inevitably present further ups and downs. This self-awareness can strengthen your ability to navigate difficulties and build greater resilience in the face of adversity.

# The Yin and Yang of challenge and joy

I've embraced a spiritual lens to my perspective on daily living. In Eastern philosophy, the concept of Yin and Yang beautifully illustrates the harmony of opposing forces. Just as day and night coexist in our daily lives, so do joy and challenge.

In the context of question three of the 5Qs Formula, 'holding space' for both the positive and the challenging aspects means that you recognise and accept that your days are a dynamic interplay of these forces. Some moments will lift you up, while other moments will offer opportunities for learning and growth. It's crucial to acknowledge and embrace this duality, especially when striving for productivity. You're not hoping for a perfect day to be productive.

Instead, you're focusing on skilfully navigating the duality of your day, embracing both the highs and lows and finding an intentional balance amid the ebb and flow of opposing forces.

## Moving from a problem-focused to solution-focused mindset

The second part of question three asks you to acknowledge what could be working better for you. Note that it is purposefully worded in this way rather than asking you, 'What is not working for you today?' Language plays a crucial role in framing your thoughts and perceptions. The wording of question three influences how you approach the question and what kind of responses it elicits from you. The question adopts a positive and proactive tone by asking what could be working better for you that day. It encourages reflection on improvement opportunities rather than focusing on shortcomings or failures. This intentional linguistic framing of the question further promotes a mindset of growth, self-awareness and solution-seeking.

In contrast, if the question was 'What is not working for you today?', it might evoke a more negative and defeatist mindset. This framing could lead to you dwelling on problems rather than seeking solutions or improvements. Being mindful and intentional about the language you use is essential when speaking to yourself, because it greatly influences your feelings and thoughts about yourself and your situation, and these in turn drive your actions and the steps you take.

This second part of question three aims to acknowledge any potential obstacles or distractions that might hinder productivity without fixating on them or allowing them to derail your entire day. By acknowledging these challenges, you're not dismissing them or pretending they don't exist. Instead, you recognise their presence and consciously choose to move forward with a positive and balanced mindset. Moreover, if appropriate or possible, you will be more inclined to look for solutions or adjustments that can be made to improve your situation. In this way, this question helps you move from a problem-focused approach to a solution-focused mindset.

## Self-compassion plays a role in achieving productivity joy

As you can read later in the chapter (see the section 'Applying the 5Qs Formula: Question three'), some of my clients' responses to this question don't include an immediate or possible solution for every challenge or situation faced. This is fine. In such cases, being compassionate to yourself and your circumstances is what is of most immediate importance and helpfulness to you. Rather than focusing on self-criticism or feelings of inadequacy when encountering challenges beyond your control, self-compassion encourages you to let go of harsh self-judgement. By developing a level of balanced acceptance of your situation, you allow yourself to move forward in that very moment.

Instead, you can adopt a gentler, more forgiving attitude toward yourself. For example, if your children have kept you awake during the night because they've been unwell, allow yourself to take regular breaks throughout the day to recharge, or plan an early evening so you can sleep earlier than usual. Rather than being overly ambitious or unrealistic in your daily goals, be compassionate to yourself by setting achievable objectives based on your limitations for that day. Or, going back to my home renovation example, I can choose to accept I'm not currently living in my dream home, but it's functional and not preventing me from doing what I really need to do. I can also remind myself of the plans in place for the home to be enhanced when the time is right. In this way, I'm not letting something I cannot change right now hinder the important and impactful things I want to achieve today.

Self-compassion is all about treating yourself with the same kindness, understanding and empathy you would offer your best friend or a loved one. It involves accepting your limitations, embracing imperfection and nurturing your wellbeing, especially when faced with challenges beyond your control and influence.

The additional value of answering question three of the 5Qs Formula lies in recognising the issues and assessing what aspects are within your control to alter or affect. Acknowledging elements you can change can enhance your motivation and provide a sense of accomplishment when you implement the adjustments and you notice an improvement. This action of implementing a change signals to yourself that you are actively taking control and assuming personal responsibility for how you respond to specific challenges or obstacles in your life. This creates a powerful mindset that nothing will defeat you and you can work around anything that comes your way.

## The subtle art of short-term compartmentalisation

Question three of the 5Qs Formula can help you develop an effective and healthy appreciation for compartmentalisation. This can allow you to manage different aspects of your life separately, often to help cope with stress, anxiety or conflicting demands. You might compartmentalise your work-related stress from your personal relationships, for example, allowing you to focus on one without being overwhelmed by the other. A healthcare professional might compartmentalise their emotions and thoughts while at work to remain objective, and then address personal worries and concerns once they are off duty. Or someone might compartmentalise personal worries while working on a challenging project to stay focused and productive on the project at hand.

I realised I had developed my skills of compartmentalisation during the pandemic when I was ten weeks into my pregnancy with my third child. Just before an important coaching call with my client, I had gotten off the phone to the hospital, because I had experienced bleeding and was concerned for the survival of my pregnancy. Despite the overwhelming fear and uncertainty I felt, I consciously decided to compartmentalise my emotions. I attended the coaching call and was fully present with my client. Before the coaching call, I said to myself, 'There is nothing I can do right now; I will only know the outcome of the pregnancy once I go to the hospital appointment'. This appointment had been scheduled in for shortly after my client call. I switched myself into a mode of being entirely work-focused and did the coaching call; my client was none the wiser and then I went to the hospital for the appointment.

Because this was during the pandemic, I had to attend the appointment on my own, and after the examination I was told the pregnancy was no longer viable. Of course, I was absolutely distraught, and the only way I could get through the devastation was by being compassionate to myself, remembering I had taken all the precautions I could have and realising this pregnancy was not meant to be. I also found solace in reminding myself to be thankful and grateful that I would soon be returning home to my two beautiful boys and husband, who were waiting to embrace me.

When I reflected on this moment, I surprised myself that I was able to compartmentalise in this way and how, by so doing, I somehow was able to navigate this personally sensitive situation with an outward appearance of composure and professionalism. I still work with this client, and we've become good friends. Three years later, I shared with him what I went through that day. He was obviously devastated to hear what I went through, and he wished he had known at the time, so that he could have postponed the coaching session or done something to support me.

While it is important to address personal and professional priorities, in some instances temporarily compartmentalising your feelings can allow you to fulfil your work obligations without compromising your productivity or quality. However, it's essential not to rely on compartmentalisation excessively or for prolonged periods. Over-reliance on this coping mechanism can hinder the integration of different aspects of your life and impede your ability to process emotions effectively and authentically.

Instead, developing the skill of compartmentalisation and using it wisely in the short term can be beneficial for navigating challenging situations. Please remember some people find it easier to compartmentalise than others, everyone is different and unique in their own strengths.

I developed my CWS strategy to help my clients compartmentalise their emotions and thoughts, and this strategy could be helpful for you too.

My CWS strategy consists of the following elements:

- *Create mental boxes:* For different aspects of life, such as work, relationships and personal challenges, have different mental boxes. When you are in a situation where you need to focus on one aspect while setting aside others, mentally place your emotions related to those other aspects into their respective boxes. If one aspect of your life is feeling very overwhelming, you can also imagine yourself locking the box for now. Visually creating these boundaries can help prevent your emotions from overwhelming you in the present moment.

- *Worry quiz:* Write down what is worrying you or consuming your energy and ask yourself a series of questions to determine its importance and whether it requires immediate action:

o   Is this something I have control over?

o   Is this something I can solve right now, or does it require further planning or preparation?

o   How likely is what I am worried about going to occur?

o   What are, if any, some of the potential solutions or steps I can take to address it right now? (There may be none, and that is fine too.)

Based on your evaluation, decide if the worry requires immediate action or can be set aside for now. For worries that require immediate action, create a brief plan to address them. For worries that can be deferred, remind yourself that you've acknowledged them and will revisit them during your next scheduled worry time.

• *Schedule worry time:* Allocate a time and place for a worry session. This could be ten to 15 minutes somewhere in your day, preferably not right before bedtime or first thing in the morning. Choose a quiet and comfortable space where you can focus without distractions. During this time, use a notebook or 'worry journal' to write down what is bothering you. This process helps externalise your worries and can provide a sense of relief by getting them out of your head and onto paper. This enables you to create distance from your worries and gain a different perspective. It can also prevent you from ruminating over distressing thoughts or feelings, which can increase levels of stress and anxiety. When you write down your worries, you're forced to organise your thoughts by putting them into words, which can help you make more sense of what you're thinking and feeling. You may even begin to think of potential solutions or coping strategies. Finally, by writing down your worries, you acknowledge your emotions and feelings in a safe and controlled environment, which can reduce their intensity and give you a sense of emotional release. This will reduce any associated anxiety or stress and improve your mood over time.

The CWS strategy can help you gain better control over your emotions and thoughts and prevent them from overwhelming you throughout the day. These tips encourage you to take a more proactive approach to problem-solving and help to reduce your anxiety and stress levels over time.

It's equally vital to engage in retrospective reflection after compartmentalisation. In chapter 9, I outline an effective end-of-day reflection exercise that allows you to acknowledge and process your emotions. This can be helpful in preventing your emotions and feelings from being dismissed or avoided—and resurfacing more intensely during times of high pressure, stress or overwhelm. In this reflection time, you may consider how well you managed to compartmentalise, what you learned about yourself and your strengths, and areas you could improve. You could reflect on how you can better manage your emotions and respond to them more effectively for future challenges. As you reflect on your emotions and experiences, practise self-compassion and kindness toward yourself. Acknowledge that feeling a range of emotions is natural, and that you are doing the best you can in challenging circumstances.

By striking this balance, you can harness the benefits of compartmentalisation while developing emotional intelligence and resilience.

In the long term, finding equilibrium between compartmentalisation and integration fosters a healthy approach to daily life, promoting productivity, joy and fulfilment. The 5Qs Formula, particularly the second part of question three, serves as a valuable tool for achieving this balance and nurturing positive psychological wellbeing and productivity.

**Self-reflection**

Can you think of a time recently where you could have benefited from using the CWS strategy? How would it have helped you? How will you remember to use the CWS strategy when you next encounter a worry that you need to compartmentalise?

# Adopting a mindset of growth and learning

The second part of question three is a catalyst to help you adopt a growth mindset, as outlined in psychologist Carol Dweck's framework of a fixed versus growth mindset. Those with a growth mindset view challenges and setbacks as opportunities for learning and development. If you have a growth mindset, you will likely believe that your abilities and capacity to do things and change things can be developed through effort, perseverance and learning from mistakes. Therefore, you are likely to approach this aspect of question three with curiosity and openness, seeing it as a chance to identify areas of improvement and look at ways to enhance your productivity.

If you lean towards a fixed mindset, believing your abilities and talents are innate and unchangeable, you might react defensively or feel threatened when confronting this aspect of question three. Instead of viewing these areas as opportunities for growth and development, you may interpret them as a reflection of your shortcomings. Or you may believe that you're already doing your best and you can't do anything else to improve your circumstances and situations and so impact your productivity positively. This fixed perspective will limit your ability to recognise the potential areas for improvement and inhibit your capacity for personal growth and development.

As an example of this, consider Shayne, who has a fixed mindset. During a performance review, his manager asks him, 'What could be working better for you?' Shayne interprets this question as a criticism of his abilities and becomes defensive. He thinks to himself, *I'm doing the best I can. If my manager thinks something needs to be better, it must mean I'm not good enough.* Instead of considering areas for improvement, Shayne dismisses the feedback and feels discouraged, believing that his abilities were fixed and unchangeable.

Conversely, Shameena has a growth mindset. During her performance review, her manager also asks Shameena, 'What could be working better for you?' Shameena views the question as an opportunity for growth and reflection. She takes a moment to consider her performance objectively and identifies areas where she could improve, such as her time management and communication skills. Shameena appreciates any feedback her manager provides, and sees the opportunity for reflection as a chance to learn and develop, recognising that her problem-solving abilities have the potential to grow.

These examples highlight that adopting a growth mindset is highly advantageous. By adopting a growth mindset wherever possible, you can develop your resiliency, and your openness to growth, feedback and continual learning, which has no glass ceiling and can feel empowering. When you are open to receiving constructive feedback, you are not disempowering yourself and giving your power over to the feedback giver. Instead, you are looking to fully understand their feedback by being open to their perspective and then deciding for yourself what insights, suggestions or learnings you choose to take forward. In this way, you become informed, empowered and hopefully equipped with what you will do next.

Remember—by engaging with both elements of question three of the 5Qs Formula, you're recognising challenges or obstacles. Similar to your response to question one, a sincere self-acknowledgement helps prevent these challenges or issues from resurfacing and affecting your mood and productivity levels throughout the day.

Additionally, question three helps you to develop your adaptability and responsiveness skills. Reflecting on what works well and what could be better improves your ability to navigate daily tasks and responsibilities. You can adjust your routine or workflows based on your self-assessment. This will allow you to respond effectively to changing circumstances and help you maintain your productivity to the best of your ability, even in challenging or changing situations.

# Applying the 5Qs Formula: Question three

As outlined through this chapter, question three of the 5Qs Formula asks you consider both what is working well and what could be working better, so let's look at how to apply each aspect in turn.

## What is working well?

When answering this part of the question, you can consider the following four categories:

- *Category one:* Acknowledge any wins, strengths or achievements you have had.

- *Category two:* Identify positive elements or aspects of your physical environment.

- *Category three:* Acknowledge positive things, interactions or events that have happened.

- *Category four:* Acknowledge positive things, interactions or events that will happen.

Your response to this part of the question can come from one or several of the four categories. These categories simply prompt you to identify what is working well for you. You only need to identify and acknowledge one or two aspects across the categories and write them down via a brief bullet point.

Here are a few example responses to this part of the question, provided by my clients who use the 5Qs Formula each day:

- *Category one:* Acknowledge any wins, strengths or achievements you have had:

  o 'I'm so pleased my team negotiated a better deal with the supplier.'

  o 'I feel my health is somewhat better than yesterday; that feels good.'

  o 'I'm happy I received excellent feedback from my boss.'

- *Category two:* Identify positive elements or aspects of your physical environment:

  o 'I'm happy the weather is bright and sunny today.'

  o 'I'm glad the home is tidy for me to focus on my work.'

  o 'I'm pleased to see that there is no washing for me to do today.'

- *Category three:* Acknowledge positive things, interactions or events that have happened:

  o 'I had a good night's sleep without my kids waking themselves or me up.'

o   'I'm so glad I could batch cook on the weekend, so I will have time to fit in a walk after work and before dinner.'

o   'I'm glad I stayed up a bit later to finish off the report last night; I feel ahead this morning.'

- *Category four:* Acknowledge positive things, interactions or events that will happen:

  o   'I've got a busy yet exciting day ahead.'

  o   'I'm so thankful we booked the holiday; I'm looking forward to it.'

  o   'I'm looking forward to my meeting with my supervisor today to get some clarity on my assignment.'

  o   'I'm looking forward to attending my son's school recital today.'

As you can read from the examples just provided, your response to this question is about noticing the small things in your daily environment or circumstances that you view as positive or working well for you. The more you notice and acknowledge these, the more you prime your brain to seek more things that you consider 'work well' for you. An accumulation of small positive things that are working well builds up to an overall feeling of positivity, joy and optimism.

Your brain will also tend to magnify and expand the things you focus on. Use this hack to your advantage by actively looking for the positives within and around you. Having a positive, optimistic mind frame will shape the lens through which you see, feel and think about your day ahead. This mind frame has the power to fuel you with hope, energy and motivation, and leads to an upbeat, 'all is possible', 'can do' attitude right from the start of your day.

Looking for small wins and positive aspects of your day that bring you joy and lift you up will serve you well. You will feel motivated to take on challenges and be resilient enough to keep going, even when things seem difficult.

When you tackle the day's challenges, you give yourself a dopamine hit, reinforcing your behaviour and giving yourself further energy and motivation to keep going. This motivation–reward cycle continues when you receive positive reinforcement by seeing your progress, and how much you've learnt or grown, and increased your self-confidence, resilience and positive feedback from others.

## What could be working better?

Some typical responses to this part of question three include the following:

- *Acknowledging a lack of sleep:* 'I didn't get enough sleep last night, and I know it might affect my focus and energy levels. However, I'm still committed to tackling my tasks to the best of my ability.'

- *Recognising external distractions:* 'I have lots of noise and activity going on around me today, which might make it harder to concentrate. Despite this, I'll find ways to create a focused work environment and stay on track.'

- *Admitting to personal concerns:* 'I'm feeling anxious about personal issues that have been on my mind lately. While they might weigh on me, I'll try to compartmentalise and stay focused on my tasks as much as possible.'

- *Experiencing technology-related challenges:* 'My internet connection has been unreliable lately, and it's frustrating when it disrupts my workflow. I'll look at putting alternative plans in place to minimise its impact so I can keep doing what needs to be done today.'

- *Recognising physical discomfort:* 'I'm dealing with some back pain today, which might make it uncomfortable to sit for long periods. However, I'll take breaks to stretch and move around, ensuring it doesn't affect my productivity too much.'

- *Acknowledging a heavy workload:* 'I have more than usual on my plate today, and it's making me feel overwhelmed. Despite the workload, I'll prioritise my tasks and break them down into manageable chunks to stay organised and focused.'

- *Admitting to a lack of motivation:* 'Honestly, I'm feeling a bit unmotivated today. It's one of those days where it's hard to get started. Nonetheless, I'll start with smaller, easier tasks to build momentum.'

- *Noticing environment distractions:* 'The construction work outside my window makes it hard to concentrate today. Although it's disruptive, I'll use noise-cancelling headphones or find a quieter space to work if possible.'

As you can see from the examples just provided, this part of question three of the 5Qs Formula enables you to identify the problems or obstacles of the day without keeping you fixated on them. You may also be able to identify ways you will overcome these obstacles.

Remember—you don't need to identify a list of all the things that are working well or could be working better each day. Simply spending one or two minutes identifying one or two specific things each day will prime your brain into a conducive, optimistic and balanced mindset to help you get the best out of your day ahead.

# Summary

Question three of the 5Qs Formula serves to intentionally prime your brain to focus on the positive aspects of your day. Directing your attention towards positive elements makes you more likely to experience positive emotions and feelings. This positivity will boost motivation, inspiration and overall happiness, making engaging with tasks and responsibilities easier and with minimal friction. Focusing on positive aspects sets the foundation for a joyous, optimistic, productive and fulfilling day ahead. When you start your day with an intentional positive mindset, you are more likely to approach challenges with resilience and creativity, contributing to greater productivity and satisfaction.

Question three facilitates a realistic assessment of what will and will not contribute to a productive day for you. By acknowledging positive elements as well as improvement areas, you gain a balanced perspective on your day. This balanced perspective is essential for decision-making and prioritisation, enabling you to navigate the complexities of your day more effectively.

Finally, question three helps you develop the beneficial skill of navigating your day's duality. By learning to identify, acknowledge and manage both highs and lows, you become better equipped to handle challenges and capitalise on opportunities, leading to greater success, productivity and fulfilment in your daily life.

# Key takeaways

- This question of the 5Qs Formula helps you intentionally hack your negativity bias daily in an effective and time-efficient way, enabling you to experience productivity joy.

- Your brain commonly deceives you in five ways. Knowing these can help you master your brain and optimise its function.

- Most people tend to perceive others' lives as more perfect or idealised than their own, a phenomenon psychologists call 'social comparison bias'.

- A momentary shift in attention from one task to another can increase the time needed to complete your main task by up to 25 per cent, due to a phenomenon known as 'switching time'.

- If you do no intentional priming, even without realising it your brain will focus on detecting things around you that it perceives to be not working well, not ideal or perfect, or not suitable for you.

- The key to responding to question three is acknowledging the small recent victories, achievements, moments or aspects of joy or positivity in your last 24 hours.

- Question three of the 5Qs Formula helps you develop an optimistic mindset. With daily practice, you will cultivate a stronger level of optimism within you, which will become a vital tool for experiencing daily productivity and joy.

- The intentional linguistic framing of question three further promotes a mindset of growth, self-awareness and solution-seeking.

- Question three helps you to develop your adaptability and responsiveness skills.

# CHAPTER 6

# Increasing productivity and joy

## *Question four: What three things do you want to achieve today?*

Question four is adored by all those who love and desire to be impactful, achieve their goals and value their time!

In this chapter, I outline the most effective methods to:

1. identify your most significant priorities for the day

2. ensure the successful completion of your tasks.

By implementing this component of the 5Qs Formula, you can experience heightened productivity and satisfaction, both in your accomplishments and how you reach them. When you feel accomplished in your day, week, month and year, life will have greater meaning and purpose to you.

Completing the initial three questions of the 5Qs Formula is akin to undertaking the invisible, inner yet crucial work of acknowledging and regulating emotions, inspiring gratitude and framing perspectives. All of these factors significantly influence the decisions you make about how you invest your time and energy. The initial questions ensure you are in the right mindset to respond appropriately to question four.

Question four will help you resist the impulse to dive straight into action. In this way, you can be intentional and confident in the purpose behind your day and what you would like to accomplish. By completing this question of the 5Qs Formula, you help ensure your valuable time and energy are always prioritised on daily high-impact, value-adding activities and tasks, which contribute to your goals.

The fourth question of the 5Qs Formula is often the question that most people want to dive straight into to commence their daily tasks promptly. This is even more accurate for those with busy schedules, who juggle numerous responsibilities and anticipate a hectic day ahead, feeling pressed for time and eager to make every moment count. However, this question has been purposefully placed towards the latter part of the 5Qs Formula sequence to encourage you to introspect first and mitigate rushing into activity and action.

As I was developing the 5Qs Formula, I noticed that many of my clients always had so much to do, and regardless of how much they had done in their day, there was still plenty left to do. This perpetual cycle of unfinished tasks left them feeling unsatisfied, often drained and frustrated with themselves. This question is not about getting everything done—as you no doubt also know, it's not possible to get everything done. Instead, it's about intentionally prioritising meaningful tasks effectively each day. By focusing on what truly matters, you'll be more productive and find genuine joy and fulfilment.

To craft and curate a life of intentionality, it's essential that all your daily actions remain aligned with your overarching vision and goals. This chapter will help you accomplish those actions each day with purpose and passion.

# Understanding why achieving tasks can be difficult

From my research into what typically hinders people from achieving what they need to do each day, I found three core key reasons:

1. Thinking patterns, such as procrastination, perfectionism, excessive overthinking or a fear of failure, can sabotage productivity.

2. Lack of clarity and connection to your purpose and goals can leave you feeling disconnected and unmotivated. Without a clear understanding of your goals and how daily tasks contribute to them, you may engage in aimless activities or prioritise tasks incorrectly. Consequently, you may end the day feeling unfulfilled.

3. Unrealistic and disjointed planning can manifest in various ways, such as setting unattainable expectations, overcommitting, or neglecting effective task prioritisation aligned with your overarching goals. Without a well organised daily plan, you can find yourself overwhelmed by your workload or uncertain about where to begin, resulting in wasted time and energy.

Question four provides an effective approach to address each of the common hindrances to productivity through three principles:

1. simplifying tasks

2. setting intentional goals and priorities

3. choosing actions that have a meaningful impact.

You will discover how to apply each of these three principles in your daily productivity in this chapter.

## Thinking patterns: Action bias, procrastination and overthinking

If you tend to jump into your daily tasks without taking a moment to plan, you might have what psychologists call an 'action bias'. This bias often stems from a need to feel productive, maintain control, or stay busy for the sake of appearing active. When driven by this urge to act quickly, you may make impulsive decisions and focus on tasks that don't align with your long-term goals. For example, instead of planning your route before leaving for work, you might rush out the door and end up taking a longer, more stressful route due to traffic or road works.

If you have an action bias, you are likely to work quickly and want to see immediate results. Seeing your progress will give you a dopamine hit and produce feelings of satisfaction and motivation to continue. Similarly, time constraints, pressure (from others, deadlines) or a fear of missing out can also influence your preference to act swiftly. You may also want to maintain control over the outcomes, which will lead you to take action without seeking input from others or delegating to others.

Contrary to an action bias, you may struggle with procrastination, delaying tasks or finding decision-making difficult. Procrastination can occur due to fear of failure, lack of motivation or feeling overwhelmed by a task. Tasks may seem daunting or overly complex, leading you to put them off until later and causing last-minute rushes to complete them. Often the first step of 'starting an activity' tends to be the hardest one to take. Remember—you don't need to take the whole staircase, just the first step!

Meet Jesse, a second-year business economics university student. Jesse has a significant research paper due at the end of his semester. Despite having several weeks to work on it, Jesse procrastinates by spending hours on social media, watching Netflix shows, or hanging out with friends. As the deadline approaches, he panics and rushes to complete his paper. He knows it will result in a lower quality submission, and he now fears the grade he will receive. Can you relate to Jesse's behaviours?

Similar to procrastination, another common obstacle to taking action is paralysis by analysis. This occurs when you're faced with too many options or information, making it hard to decide what to do. Spending time in excessive overthinking and too much time weighing up possibilities can lead to missed opportunities, looming deadlines and increased stress. Can you recall a time when you felt stuck like this?

It happened to Paul and Mike recently. They are parents to two wonderful primary school–aged twin boys. They were trying to decide on the best educational approach for their children, choosing between private, public and even homeschooling. They spent countless hours researching different educational philosophies, reading reviews of schools, attending open evenings, spending money to put their children's names on the various school waitlists, and consulting with other parents.

Despite having the desire and motivation to provide the best education option for their twin boys, they found themselves unable to decide due to the overwhelming amount of information and their fear of making the wrong decision. As a result, their children's education choices were at risk of being reduced, and both the parents and the children experienced a high level of stress and anxiety with all the uncertainty and indecisiveness. Thankfully, they did eventually make a decision, and they and the boys felt so much better by having certainty and knowing what the future would look like for the next phase of their lives. Moving past paralysis by analysis unlocks progress.

Another example is my client Amar, a fabulously smart, highly ambitious and competitive digital app business owner. Amar and his team wanted to expand their product line to reach a broader market. They spent weeks researching different product ideas, market trends and potential suppliers. They became deeply engrossed in analysing every aspect of the expansion and struggled to decide which digital product to go with. The fear of making the wrong decision and an extensive period of analysis and decision-making led to significant delays in launching a new product. Unfortunately, this in turn led to missed opportunities, a loss of new revenue and decreased team morale. Recognising the negative impact of their approach, Amar and his team reflected on their decision-making approaches, fears and mindset, and, together, we worked on shifting their mindset to cultivate a more proactive and confident approach to innovation and expansion.

## Moving to an 'impact' orientation

As illustrated by the examples just provided, both procrastination and paralysis by analysis can get the best of you at the worst times and hinder progress, particularly when you least expect it. Having strategies in place to overcome unproductive thinking patterns is essential, enabling you to take deliberate action and enhance your productivity.

The optimal thinking orientation is one of 'impact', where you are continually proactive to drive results, and focused on outcomes that make a positive difference. For example, my client Susan is an impact-oriented individual who works as a community organiser. Instead of merely attending meetings, she takes proactive steps to address pressing issues in her neighbourhood. When she noticed a lack of access to affordable childcare, for example, she rallied community members, liaised with local authorities and spearheaded a campaign to establish a subsidised childcare centre. Through her actions, Susan demonstrates her commitment to making a tangible difference in the lives of others and the overall wellbeing of her community.

Similarly, Pritesh, a finance leader at a multinational corporation, is also an impact-driven leader. Rather than focusing on routine financial reporting and budget management, he is always trying to identify opportunities to streamline processes within the finance department. Pritesh led a team to implement automated financial systems, for example, resulting in significant time and cost savings for the company. Additionally, he recognises the importance of sustainable finance practices and spearheads initiatives to integrate environmental, social and governance (ESG) considerations into the company's investment strategies. Through his strategic leadership and innovative approach, Pritesh not only enhances the efficiency of financial operations, but also drives positive impact by promoting responsible financial practices.

## Self-reflection

Understanding whether you tend to be action-orientated, to procrastinate or overthink, or be impact-orientated is essential to implementing effective strategies that will help you be productive and experience joy.

1. In the table provided, tick which of each response *most* applies to you across each of the three columns. (Or highlight if using an ebook.)

2. Count the number of ticks or highlights in each column. The column with the most ticks likely represents your typical tendency.

*(continued)*

However, remember that this could vary depending on the tasks you are required to complete each day and your mindset while answering the orientation quiz below.

**Orientation quiz**

| Action orientation | Procrastination orientation | Overthinking orientation | Impact orientation |
|---|---|---|---|
| I tend to make decisions quickly and take immediate action. | I frequently delay starting tasks or projects until the last minute. | I tend to overthink decisions and get stuck in the analysis without taking action. | I consistently seek ways to create a positive change or make a positive difference. |
| I am comfortable with uncertainty and willing to take calculated risks. | I struggle to stay focused and easily get distracted by non-essential activities. | I find it challenging to make decisions, even when I have sufficient information. | I am driven by the desire to achieve tangible results or outcomes. |
| I prioritise getting things done and achieving results over perfection. | I often find excuses to avoid acting on important or high-impact tasks. | I fear making the wrong decision and worry about the potential consequences. | I prioritise tasks and activities based on their potential impact or contribution to larger goals. |
| I feel energised and motivated by tackling new challenges and projects. | I experience feelings of guilt or anxiety about procrastinating on tasks. | I struggle to move forward on projects, initiatives or tasks due to indecision or perfectionism. | I actively seek opportunities to innovate, solve problems or improve existing processes. |
| I am often praised for my ability to take initiative and drive projects forward. | I frequently underestimate the time required to complete tasks or overestimate my ability to complete them quickly. | I often feel overwhelmed or stuck when faced with multiple options or decisions, leading to difficulty in making choices or taking action. | I am motivated by the potential long-term effects or benefits of my actions, rather than short-term gratification. |

3. Identify which orientation you currently are in and highlight the relevant quadrant in the following Orientation matrix. In this figure, the *y*-axis represents low action to high action, and the *x*-axis represents low impact to high impact.

4. Identify which orientation you desire to be and highlight the relevant quadrant in the figure.

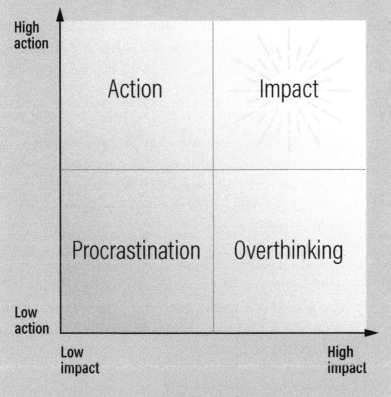

**Orientation matrix**

Completing this self-reflection exercise can give you valuable insight into your typical tendencies and approaches to productivity and decision-making. By identifying whether you are action-oriented, prone to procrastination or overthinking, or impact-oriented, you can better understand your behaviour patterns and potential barriers to productivity. The path to success is to first understand yourself.

## Overcoming your thinking patterns

Once you've determined your current productivity orientation through the self-reflection exercise in the preceding section, you can start to make changes corresponding to your current and desired orientation. Keep in mind that to live intentionally and with impact each day, you need to strive for a high-impact orientation in your thinking, approach and execution as much as possible.

Here are a few helpful and practical tips to use throughout your day to help you overcome the potential barriers in each of the first three orientations, and move towards an impact orientation.

Action-orientation:

- *Practise strategic procrastination:* This involves delaying action on tasks that have a lower impact, or can be delegated to others. By postponing low-impact tasks, you can free up time and energy to do more meaningful and impactful activities.

- *Set boundaries:* Establish boundaries around your time and commitments to avoid overcommitting yourself. Learn to say no to tasks or activities that do not align with your goals or priorities. (Guidance on how to say no is provided later in this chapter.)

- *Pause and reflect:* Before jumping into action, take a moment to pause and reflect on the task at hand. Give yourself a second chance to reconsider whether it has a high impact and aligns with your goals, or whether there might be a more efficient or effective way to approach it.

Procrastination orientation:

- *Chunk tasks:* Break tasks, especially larger ones, into smaller chunks. This makes the tasks more manageable and less intimidating and easier to start.

- *Use the Pomodoro Technique:* This is where you work in short, focused bursts and then have a quick break—for example, 25 minutes of work, followed by a five-minute break. This can help you maintain productivity momentum and combat procrastination.

- *Create a reward system:* Set up a reward system to incentivise you to complete tasks. By breaking your tasks into smaller milestones, you can reward yourself each time you achieve one. The rewards can be small treats, enjoyable activities or anything that motivates you.

Overthinking orientation:

- *Set time limits for decision-making:* Give yourself a specific time frame to weigh up options and a deadline to make a decision (even if it's an artificial deadline and you treat it like a real one!). This will help you avoid excessive rumination.

- *Set limits on collecting information:* If you find yourself continuously seeking more information or reassurance before making a decision, set limits on how much time you will spend gathering information and be clear on the criteria for choosing the information you need. Once you've collected the information based on your criteria, trust yourself to make a decision and take action.

- *Focus on solutions:* Instead of dwelling on worst-case scenarios, shift your focus to solutions and move forward. Break down complex problems into manageable steps and focus on what you can control, rather than what you can't.

Impact orientation:

- *Define your goals and values:* Take the time to establish clear goals (covered later in this chapter) and clarify your values (discussed in chapter 7). By completing question four of the 5Qs Formula every day, you're regularly reflecting on what matters most to you and identifying where you can contribute meaningfully each day.

- *Focus on action and results:* Shift your mindset from simply going through the motions to actively seek opportunities to create impact and make a positive difference (similar to the Susan and Pritesh examples included in the previous section). Prioritise tasks and projects based on their potential to generate tangible outcomes and focus your efforts on activities that align with your goals.

- *Develop learning agility:* Continuously reflect on what is and isn't working, and remain receptive to fresh ideas, perspectives and opportunities for growth. Be willing to adapt your approach on feedback and lessons learnt, to help you create a positive impact sooner and more often. (Question five, covered in the next chapter, also helps you focus on this area.)

While each of the first three orientations has pros and cons, neither alone will help you achieve your optimal daily productivity. This can only be achieved through practising the impact orientation.

However, once you identify your current orientation, you can work on managing it more by implementing the tips just provided. Don't despair if your current orientation is not where you would like it to be. Now that you have greater awareness, you can take practical steps to move toward your desired orientation, and toward higher impact and higher action.

Question four of the 5Qs Formula helps you focus on 'considered' action and prevents feelings of overwhelm from a never-ending daily to-do list. As part of pausing and reflecting at the beginning of your day for only five minutes, you can intentionally select three high-impact tasks to focus on that align with your broader purpose and goals.

## Clarity on purpose and goals

Every year, our family goes on what we fondly refer to as 'The Annual Rayat Retreat'. During this retreat, my husband, our boys and I escape to a remote countryside location, immersing ourselves in nature and disconnecting from the hustle of daily life. Many of my corporate clients, effective leaders and business owners hold strategic offsite conferences and retreats, and this is what inspired us. Our family retreat provides invaluable headspace for clear, expansive thinking, opportunities for meaningful connections and essential time to recharge as a family.

We usually pack our bathers, loungewear and, of course, whiteboards, flipcharts, sticky notes and colourful sharpies. We spend this quality time immersed together, relaxing and having fun but also reflecting on the year just passed, as we share our learnings and celebrate our achievements. We then focus on identifying our individual goals for the year. We each come up with three to five individual goals, and then we talk about what each of us needs to do, each day, to achieve those goals, what support we need from each other and also what behaviours we need to demonstrate each day to achieve our goals. We also come up with three collective family goals we can all commit to.

This strategic family planning isn't just for the benefit of us adults. My husband and I want our children to learn the importance of life by design, and to be conscious and intentional about their choices and the possibilities they set for themselves. In this way, they will learn the vital skill of establishing their own SMART (specific, measurable, achievable, relevant and time-bound) goals, and they will feel empowered, supported and encouraged to reach for things they consider important. I can easily still see my boys' faces, as they excitedly share their goals, write them on sticky notes and then over the next few days really think and discuss the ways in which they are going to work towards their goals. I really love hearing their goals; at the age of five, my youngest once shared that he wanted to be the best helper at home and keep his bedroom tidy!

Whether my family and I achieve every one of our individual or collective audacious goals or not, we are all committed to the promise of growth, improvement and intentional living, and we are in it together to support one another.

Leadership and business strategist Greg McKeown talks about the concept of an 'essential intent' in his book *Essentialism*. He shares that it is important to have a clear focus, goal or purpose that you are working towards. In this way, you focus your time each day on the tasks that will contribute directly to your goal and what truly matters to you. He shares that by doing so, you remove the clutter or noise of all irrelevant tasks, and so feel less stressed. Life is less chaotic, and you can stop constantly 'putting out fires' and doing things that won't help you achieve your goals.

Do you have a big goal you want to achieve? Perhaps you want to write a book, secure a promotion, be recognised for an award, publish your research, complete your degree, or purchase a new home. You may have a few goals, related to different aspects of your life. I recommend setting a clear goal for each aspect of your life.

The different areas in your life, and the goals within them, could include the following:

- *Professional:* Career advancement or business growth goals, skills development, networking and contributions to your field or industry.

- *Personal development:* Learning new skills, gaining knowledge, expanding perspectives and developing self-awareness.

- *Health and fitness:* Maintaining and improving physical and mental wellbeing through exercise, nutrition, stress management and quality sleep.

- *Family:* Spending quality time, offering support and sharing new experiences.

- *Relationships:* Connecting and creating memories with loved ones and friends, old and new.

## Self-reflection

1. Take a moment to clarify your major goals for the upcoming six to 12 months. Don't feel restricted by waiting for a specific time of year to do this exercise — begin the process today.

*(continued)*

2.  Close your eyes and envision what you would like to have accomplished if you fast-forwarded 12 months from now and reflected on your achievement. What you would like to say and feel about each aspect of your life, and what do you hope has changed or even stayed the same?

3.  Once you've identified these desired changes, jot them down as your goals to focus on in the next six to 12 months. Then, transform these goals into SMART goals (specific, measurable, achievable, relevant and time-bound) and write them clearly in your journal and have them easily accessible for you to view.

Being a visual person, I also find it helpful to capture my goals as images and words, and I often create an electronic vision board that clearly displays my goals. I then store the vision board as my laptop desktop background. This way, I can be easily reminded of my goals each time I use my laptop, and the goals can stay front and centre of my attention too. You may wish to also try this.

Being clear on your longer term goals helps give you focus, clarity and motivation to prioritise your time to identify and complete three meaningful and purposeful high-impact tasks each day. So when you think of your top three tasks for the day, also consider your long-term goals. For example, if your goal is to be the best basketball player you can be, one of your daily tasks must be practising basketball.

To ensure productivity during your workday, it's crucial to recognise that while you have goals for various aspects of your life, you will also likely have specific work goals. If you are employed by someone else, these will have been established through mutual agreement between you and your manager. Having clarity regarding your work goals will enable you to align your daily tasks accordingly, and this alignment will facilitate a productive workday.

For example, Harpreet works as a software engineer at a tech company. Her personal and professional goals include mastering new programming languages and eventually transitioning into a leadership role. However, her current work goals, established in collaboration with her manager, involve developing a new feature for the company's flagship software product. Harpreet ensures that her daily tasks contribute directly to her personal growth *and* the project's success. She does this by aligning her aspirations with the specific work goal of developing the new software feature. This alignment enhances her productivity and progress towards her career objectives.

Life often pulls you in too many directions, and your daily tasks may not contribute to your bigger goals. Therefore, question four of the 5Qs Formula serves as a good daily reminder to consider and intentionally select daily tasks that are aligned with your goals.

## Realistic and aligned planning for daily accomplishment

Question four of the 5Qs Formula aims to set you up for success by encouraging you to identify only three tasks to achieve in a day—not five, ten or 20, only three!

Research suggests that identifying three specific tasks each day and writing them down can greatly improve focus, intentionality and commitment to completion. By narrowing your to-do list to three tasks, you can concentrate your efforts more effectively, reducing the overwhelm and stress of a lengthy to-do list.

Long daily to-do lists are likely to increase your cortisol levels because they can feel overwhelming and lead to stress rather than motivation. The feelings of overwhelm and stress can take over, and you can unnecessarily waste your energy as you focus on worrying about how you will get through your long list rather than being fully present on each task at a time. Often, a long daily to-do list is simply a list of tasks that lacks any order of prioritisation, making it difficult to know where to start. When you don't know where to start, you can stall your intention to start any tasks, leading to procrastination or indecisiveness, which, as described earlier in the chapter, can make it even harder to get things done. Also, having a long daily to-do list makes it harder to see how particular tasks align with specific goals you are trying to achieve. Similar to tasks that are not prioritised, doing specific tasks can feel meaningless if they are not connected to a bigger goal.

The 'rule of three' memory retention phenomenon supports this approach. This rule works on the premise that your brain's working memory can handle three tasks or priorities at a time, and sticking to this number makes it easier to maintain focus and adapt to incoming requests or unexpected events. Similarly, grouping information in threes helps your brain recognise and remember patterns, providing clarity and control over your daily tasks. Three is the smallest number needed to create a pattern. For example, classic storytelling always has a beginning, middle and end. In everyday life, frameworks are often captured in a three-part structure—for example, the traffic light system of 'red, amber, green', instructions such as 'ready, set, go' or 'stop, look and listen', or reflection models such as 'stop, start, continue'. By grouping information in threes, your brain is likely to better recognise and remember patterns, giving you greater control and clarity on what you need and want to achieve on a given day.

By identifying three priorities at the start of each day, you also reaffirm the value you place on your time, set clear boundaries for yourself and others, and prioritise only high-impact tasks. Once your three tasks are completed to the best of your ability and the expectation required, the rest of the time in your day is yours to choose what you want to do—perhaps a reward or a hobby, or spending time with your loved ones. Or perhaps you can use the time to work on your own professional development, which, in turn, will help you in your business, your career and your personal relationships.

While at initial glance this approach may seem limiting or impossible given the numerous tasks you face daily, adopting a strict discipline to prioritise three key tasks each day can truly yield remarkable results. By consistently selecting three tasks daily, you're setting yourself up to accomplish 15 significant high-impact tasks by the end of a full workweek and a whopping 60 high-impact tasks by the end of a full month.

Indeed, having a planner and strategising ahead (over the coming weeks, months and even year) can provide a sense of structure and direction. Question four, used as a daily tool, emphasises the importance of aligning short-term actions with long-term goals across various facets of your life. By focusing on three-high impact tasks daily, you can ensure that your daily efforts contribute meaningfully to your overarching goals.

Consistently executing these mini daily plans allows for steady progress towards long-term goals. Over time, this accumulation of completed tasks leads to the fulfilment of your broader purpose and the achievement of your goals.

## Spend time on creating impact and having purpose

Question four serves as a potent reminder that time is finite. Time is essentially the rarest commodity we have. Therefore, it's crucial to invest your time wisely in tasks that create impact and serve a purpose each day.

When deciding on the three tasks to focus on each day, it's essential to evaluate their impact. Consider what positive difference or change completing each task will bring to yourself or others. This means selecting activities or tasks that will bring about a positive change and provide value to yourself, your family, your organisation or its customers. Choose three high-impact tasks aligned with the long-term goals you previously identified (refer to the section 'Clarity on purpose and goals', earlier in this chapter). High-impact daily tasks should aim to save time, energy and effort or to enhance experiences, quality, sense of achievement and overall wellbeing.

Here are a few examples of high-impact tasks that link to some common overarching goals:

- *Goal:* Improve physical health.

  o *High-impact task:* Complete a 30-minute workout session focusing on cardio and strength training.

- *Goal:* Get a promotion.

  o *High-impact task:* Create a document to communicate your achievements and contributions to your manager, highlighting how your work has positively impacted key metrics or contributed to the overall success of projects or objectives.

- *Goal:* Strengthen relationship with partner.

  o *High-impact task:* Schedule and spend quality time with your partner, having a meaningful conversation or doing something fun together.

- *Goal:* Develop a high-performing team.

  o *High-impact task:* Conduct regular one-to-one catch-ups with team to find out what motivates them and how they can be set up for success.

## *Breaking down tasks*

At times your high-impact tasks can be sizeable, meaning they are unlikely to be completed in a single day—for example, a large project or a complex task. The sub-tasks for this overall task then need to be prioritised within your three high-impact tasks, across multiple days, weeks or even months, depending on their size, complexity and your time frame for completion.

For example, let's say your overall task is to develop a marketing plan for a new company product. Given that this is a sizeable task, you need to break the task into more manageable high-impact tasks and sub-tasks. This approach makes the overall task less overwhelming and allows you to make progress incrementally. By breaking down the task into smaller components, all of which are high-impact tasks, you can create a clear roadmap for developing your marketing plan.

Here's how you might break this overall task down:

- *Overall task:* Develop marketing plan for new product.

  o *High-impact task:* Conduct market research.

    ▪ *Sub-task:* Research competitors.

    ▪ *Sub-task:* Identify gaps and opportunities in the market where competitors may be lacking.

  o *High-impact task:* Meet with key stakeholders.

    ▪ *Sub-task:* Discuss project goals, objectives and expectations.

    ▪ *Sub-task:* Gather insights and input from stakeholders to inform the development of the marketing plan.

o   *High-impact task:* Define target audience.

- *Sub-task:* Identify demographic characteristics, lifestyle habits, values and attitude of target audience.

- *Sub-task:* Segment the target audience into distinct groups based on their needs, preferences and behaviours.

As you can see from this breakdown, only high-impact tasks have been selected to be prioritised in relation to the overall task of developing a marketing plan. Similarly, smaller yet still high-impact tasks have been prioritised for the overall task. This demonstrates the effectiveness of breaking down sizable tasks into smaller, more manageable sub-tasks.

Remember—each time a task is broken down, questioning whether the sub-task remains of high impact is essential. While a sub-task may be crucial in the short term, its long-term impact should also be considered.

Prioritising tasks based on their immediate importance is equally valid and necessary for progress. For example, imagine you have an overall task of cleaning your entire house. One high-impact task could be to clean the kitchen. Within this task, a sub-task might be to wash the dishes. While washing the dishes may not directly contribute to the long-term cleanliness of the entire house, it's necessary to prioritise this in the short term to prevent a build-up of dirty dishes and maintain a functional kitchen.

Tracking your progress as you complete each sub-task not only makes the process more manageable but also provides a sense of accomplishment and motivation as you move closer to achieving your ultimate goal. Remember—high-impact tasks are essential tasks that must be prioritised to progress towards your goal.

Of course, certain mundane, regular tasks will still need to be done; however, you can look to complete them around your three high-impact tasks. For example, as a parent, it's important to ensure that household chores such as laundry, dishes and cleaning are completed regularly to maintain a clean and organised home environment. While these tasks are essential for daily living and family wellbeing, they may not significantly impact your child's long-term development or emotional wellbeing. So you might prioritise spending quality time with your child, playing, learning and having meaningful conversations, and complete the household chores as a family around these or, if possible, outsource such tasks.

Or as a business owner, overseeing and managing your business's day-to-day operations, such as monitoring finances, undertaking administrative and compliance tasks and addressing immediate operational issues, is essential for the business's smooth running. However, such tasks do not directly contribute to driving growth or innovation, in the same way as developing a marketing plan or strategic vision would have the potential to do. These tasks are part of a business owner's responsibility because they contribute to operational efficiency. However, prioritising high-impact daily tasks will increase satisfaction and fulfilment while reducing resentment towards perceived mundane tasks.

## Self-reflection

Take five minutes to write down as many tasks as you can remember from your current day. Then highlight the highly impactful ones — the tasks that had the most significant impact on your day or progress towards one of your goals.

(continued)

Reflect on these questions:

1.  What approximate percentage of tasks that you did was of high impact in your day?

2.  Were there any tasks that were time-sensitive or particularly urgent, but of low impact?

3.  Which tasks did you enjoy doing? Which did you loath doing or feel okay about?

The purpose of this brief reflection exercise is to develop your awareness of how you spend your time. This reflection encourages you to be more intentional and strategic in your task management, which will lead to greater productivity and joy.

## Combining impact and urgency

To best focus on identifying your three high-impact tasks each day, I recommend using my adapted version of the well-known Eisenhower Method, with an adapted focus on impact and urgency. (The Eisenhower Method uses a matrix based on importance and urgency.)

Using the word 'impact' here is a great reminder to spend time on things that can add value and make a positive difference to you and others, rather than focusing on things that are important to get done but not impactful. For example, your company may require all its employees to attend a monthly 'all hands' meeting. While your attendance is important for staying informed about the company's updates and aligning with team goals, the content discussed in these meetings may not directly impact your day-to-day work or contribute directly to your personal or professional growth.

From your responses to the preceding self-reflection exercise, you no doubt see that important tasks are not always of high impact. The key is differentiating which are your most highly impactful tasks and ensuring you tackle and prioritise these first. The Impact versus Urgency matrix in the following figure helps you identify which tasks to prioritise.

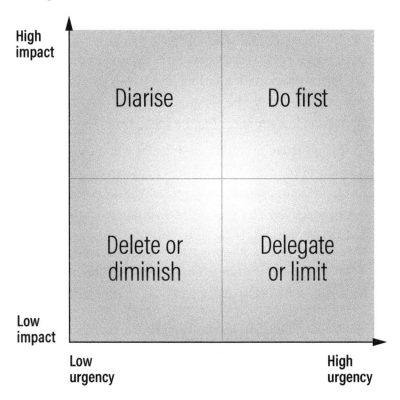

**Impact versus Urgency matrix**

### High impact and high urgency: Do first

These tasks require immediate attention because they contribute significantly to your goals or have time sensitive deadlines. For example, such tasks might include:

- drafting a proposal for a major client presentation scheduled for later that day

- resolving a client or customer feedback issue

- studying for an upcoming final exam that will heavily influence your overall grade

- attending a parent–teacher meeting to address concerns about your child's academic performance or wellbeing at school

- addressing a crisis situation within the organisation that threatens its reputation or financial stability.

## High impact and low urgency: Diarise these tasks

Tasks in this quadrant are value adding and will make a difference but don't require an immediate action. They contribute significantly to your longer term success or objectives, so schedule time to address these tasks proactively and prevent them from becoming urgent in the future. Such tasks might include:

- researching and planning for a new marketing campaign that will launch next quarter

- developing a long-term business growth strategy to expand into new markets over the next year

- planning a family holiday to create lasting memories during school holidays.

## Low impact and high urgency: Delegate or limit

Tasks in this quadrant are urgent but don't contribute to your goals or long-term success. They often demand immediate attention but offer little value in the grand scheme of things. Look to delegate these tasks to others or limit the time spent on them so you can focus on more impactful activities. An example here might be handling sibling squabbles by setting clear boundaries and enabling children to resolve conflicts independently where possible or outsourcing various household chores and tasks to relevant others, to free up your time for high-impact tasks.

## Low impact and low urgency: Delete or diminish

Tasks in this quadrant are neither value adding nor urgent. They are time wasters that distract from your goals and should be deleted or diminished where possible. These tasks include the following:

- mindlessly scrolling social media

- organising office supplies or rearranging office furniture (although I must say I love ordering new stationary and quite like changes in my environment)

- watching television or playing video games for long periods of time

- engaging in office gossip or politics or unnecessary meetings that drain time and energy.

## Prioritising

When you identify your three tasks, where possible, try to prioritise the tasks that fall into this order of quadrants: high-impact, high-urgency quadrant, followed by low-impact, high-urgency quadrant, followed by high-impact, low-urgency. Finally, question whether you really need to do the tasks that follow in the low-impact, low-urgency quadrant.

Examples of some of the high-impact and high-urgency tasks my clients have captured previously include, in no particular order:

- client presentations

- unwell child

- assignment deadlines

- exams

- health appointments

- proposal and submission deadlines

- business development meetings

- creating shareable value-add content

- writing a business case

- celebrating wins, milestones and progress

- helping children with a school project

- one-on-ones with the team.

Keep in mind that, in relation to your personal goals, you're the best judge of what tasks are high-impact and urgent.

Depending on your profession, position and circumstances, you may have limited autonomy in prioritising your work tasks. But it's crucial to understand each task's potential impact, to make a positive difference and the value it will bring. If you are unsure, talk with the person who assigned it to you to confirm its impact. This will ensure you have a clear understanding of the task and confirmation of its value. Often tasks are assigned out of habit without questioning their true value-add.

Remember—the beauty of question four is that once your three high-impact tasks are done, the rest of your day is available. You can then choose what else and how else you spend your time.

Now if you're a high achiever or accustomed to constant busyness, it can be challenging to halt work once the three most impactful tasks for the day are completed. Your position and circumstance may also mean you can't 'down tools' completely. However, stopping doesn't necessarily mean complete cessation of any activity or tasks; rather it signifies freeing yourself of guilt or pressure to continually do more (often imposed on ourselves by ourselves!). This realisation can be liberating, particularly if you are accustomed to perpetual action. By adopting this approach, you can be more present, ultimately achieving greater impact with fewer tasks. This mindset shift is integral to living an intentional, productive and fulfilling life. It involves making space and time for activities that generate high impact, provide value, bring enjoyment, and evoke a sense of fulfilment on completion.

## Allocating time for your tasks

After identifying your three high-impact tasks, it's essential to plan when you'll tackle each one. Use a physical or electronic diary to organise your schedule. Review your calendar to make room for your priority (high-impact) tasks by replacing the low-impact ones.

Allocate 60- to 90-minute time blocks for each high-impact task and block out the time in your calendar so it's visible to you and anyone else who accesses your calendar to ensure focused and uninterrupted work. Anticipate future commitments by reviewing your schedule a week or two in advance, allowing flexibility to adjust as needed.

Set yourself a deadline—even an artificial deadline—for each task, to help you maintain focus and efficiency.

You may have heard the saying, 'If you want something done, ask a busy person to do it'. This highlights that busy people, such as working parents or those wearing multiple hats, are often the most effective at managing tasks because they have honed their time management skills and learnt how to prioritise responsibilities. I know you've got this!

As an example, in my role as a senior organisational psychologist at a communications marketing company in London, I negotiated a working arrangement with my manager to balance my parental responsibilities when my child started nursery (similar to child or day care in Australia). We agreed that I would leave the office by 5 pm daily to pick up my son, despite the usual office hours extending to 6 pm. With reduced time during the day, I focused intensely during office hours, collaborating efficiently with my team and clients. I prioritised essential tasks and meetings to maximise productivity within the set time frame. The need to leave promptly at 5 pm drove me to manage my time ruthlessly and complete as much of my work, which involved collaborating with others, in those set hours.

After putting my son to bed, I would spend an hour in the evening tying up loose ends and responding to emails. This schedule taught me valuable time management lessons and helped me develop a disciplined approach to balancing work and family life. Setting boundaries and valuing my time wisely became essential especially during this phase in my life.

In many workplaces, the implicit expectation is often to prioritise work above all else, leading some employees to feel guilty or inadequate if they cannot prioritise work over personal responsibilities. I coached a high-performing executive who felt pressured by societal norms to stay late at work, because she did not have personal responsibilities such as child or pet care. I challenged her beliefs and conforming to societal norms, highlighting it is important for organisations to promote cultures that respect individuals' boundaries and value their time outside of work equally, regardless if they have caring responsibilities or not. From our work together, she achieved a more sustainable and balanced approach to productivity based on impact and valuing her own time, which led to greater satisfaction and effectiveness in her personal and professional life. Being one of the leaders in the organisation, she also role-modelled this behaviour and set a tone for a healthier approach to work and personal life for others in the organisation too.

## Self-reflection

Can you identify any societal expectations or norms that may be influencing your productivity?

Here are some of the common societal norms or expectations I hear from my clients, along with the ways they can affect productivity:

- The belief that productivity is solely measured by long hours at work, which can lead to you feeling guilty for taking breaks or prioritising self-care.

- The pressure to constantly be available and responsive, even during non-working hours, due to the expectation of instant communication via online platforms, which can again reduce self-care and increase stress.

- The notion that multi-tasking is necessary for success, which leads to fragmented attention and decreased efficiency.

- The stigma surrounding asking for help or delegation, which can make you feel as if you must handle all tasks independently, even if it leads to burnout.

- The emphasis on busyness as a status symbol, which can compel you to fill your schedule with tasks and commitments to appear successful or important.

If faced with any of these norms or expectations, consider how you may challenge them to enable you to accommodate your personal needs and goals better.

## *Getting better at saying no*

Question four helps you establish your daily priorities by identifying three high-impact tasks, signalling your focus and agenda firstly to yourself and then to others. Having a clear agenda makes it less likely that others will successfully sway you toward their goals, because you're already committed to your own. Without a plan, you're more susceptible to being pulled into fulfilling others' needs and more likely to neglect your own.

Clarity about your agenda also helps in communicating your priorities to others, particularly if you struggle with saying no due to a tendency to please others. As Brené Brown advises, 'Set boundaries even if it's at the risk of disappointing others'. Question four empowers you to do just that.

When respectfully declining work requests, consider incorporating the following:

- Communicate your current priorities to provide insight into your workload. This transparency helps both you and others make informed decisions about task allocations and time lines.

- Ask questions about the requested task, including expertise required, time lines and expectations, and discuss potential alternatives for delegation. This demonstrates your willingness to consider the task, while also managing your workload effectively.

Here are some helpful responses or phrases you could use in situations where you don't have the time to prioritise others' requests:

- 'I appreciate you considering me for this task. Given my current workload, I believe it would be more effective for someone else to pick this up, unless it can wait till next week.'

- 'I understand the importance of this task *and* given my current workload, I won't be able to complete it in time. Let's explore how else or who else can complete the task.'

Notice the use of 'and' in the second example—using the word 'but' can put people offside, while 'and' keeps the conversation collaborative and inclusive. Respectfully and clearly communicating no to requests you don't see as value-adding or do not have the time to complete is an effective way to manage your productivity, wellbeing, and sense of influence and control over your time.

Even if you are not a people-pleaser, you may still find yourself in environments where you are instructed to perform many low-impactful tasks. Meet my client Alex, who experienced just this. Alex was a project manager at a busy tech start-up, where demands were constantly shifting and new tasks seemed to pile up every day. Despite Alex's meticulous planning and focus on high-impact projects, he found himself overwhelmed by requests for minor updates and unnecessary meetings, and the completion of administrative tasks that ate away at his time.

Feeling frustrated and stretched thin, Alex decided to take action. He started by assessing his workload and identifying the tasks that truly mattered in moving the company forward. Armed with this clarity, he scheduled a meeting with his team and his supervisor to discuss his priorities and the challenges he faced. During the meeting, Alex diplomatically and respectfully explained how the volume of non-essential tasks was hindering his ability to focus on critical projects. He provided concrete examples and data to illustrate the impact these distractions were having on overall productivity and project time lines.

Rather than simply complaining, Alex then proposed practical solutions. He suggested streamlining communication channels, delegating certain tasks to team members who were better suited for them, and implementing a more structured approach to task prioritisation.

To Alex's surprise, both his team and his supervisor were receptive to his concerns. They acknowledged the validity of his points and agreed to implement some of his suggestions. Together, they developed a plan to reduce unnecessary tasks and streamline workflows, allowing Alex to focus his time and energy on projects that truly mattered. As a result of Alex's initiative and assertiveness, the team saw a noticeable improvement in overall productivity and morale. With fewer distractions and a clearer focus on high-impact tasks, they were all able to achieve their goals more efficiently and effectively.

## Regularly scrutinise your diary

Get into the habit of regularly reviewing your diary, preferably at least one week in advance, to carefully assess each scheduled meeting or activity. This simple practice should only require ten to 15 minutes of your time. Ask yourself, 'What value do I contribute by attending this meeting? Is my presence essential?' Similarly, evaluate your tasks and activities. Are they still relevant and aligned with your goals? Are they of high impact? Do they truly require your attention?

By scrutinising your diary in this manner at the beginning and end of each week, you can ensure that only necessary and high-impact tasks occupy your valuable time and energy. This proactive approach to managing your schedule can lead to increased productivity, focus and effectiveness in achieving your goals.

Also consider whether you have the flexibility to structure your day in line with your energy. If you have such flexibility, prioritise completing high-impact tasks during times when you feel more energised, creative and focused. Author Daniel Pink, in his book *When: The Scientific Secrets of Perfect Timing*, and leading neuroscientist Dr Andrew Huberman both emphasise the importance of identifying peak productivity periods within your day.

During my university days in Nottingham in the United Kingdom, completing my masters in organisational psychology in 2004, I discovered that my peak focus hours were in the mornings from 8 am to 12 noon and again between 7 pm and 10 pm. Leveraging these peak periods, I structured my study revision and assignments accordingly, allowing me to reserve the middle of the day for enjoyable activities such as reading, shopping, exercising and socialising with my friends. Initially, it felt counterintuitive to step away from constant studying, especially leading up to my exams. However, I soon realised that studying during periods of low energy and scattered focus was detrimental to both my productivity and the quality of my revision.

Now, as a working mother managing a bustling household, I prioritise my work around my availability, often completing tasks while my children are at school to ensure I can fully engage with them after school. Like many of my clients facing similar challenges, I no longer have the luxury of working during my peak energy times; instead, my schedule revolves around my children's school hours. This necessity is partly what led me to develop the 5Qs Formula, aimed at helping individuals optimise their energy and focus levels to accomplish meaningful, high-impact work whenever possible.

# Applying the 5Qs Formula: Question four

To best focus on identifying your three high-impact tasks each day, follow these four simple steps:

1.  Begin by revisiting your goals for the next six to 12 months to align your daily tasks with your long-term objectives.

2. List all the tasks you believe you should or would like to accomplish today. Then utilise the adapted Impact versus Urgency matrix to categorise these tasks into quadrants

3. Focus on tasks in the 'Do first' and 'Diarise' quadrants. From these, select your top three tasks that will be the primary focus of your day.

4. Block out three separate 60- to 90-minute intervals for each of your three high-impact tasks in your calendar.

Keep in mind that certain tasks may be substantial and require more than the allocated 60 to 90 minutes to complete. In such instances, break down these sizeable tasks into a series of manageable sub-tasks. Ensure that at least one sub-task is designated as one of your three high-impact tasks for the day. By dividing larger tasks into smaller, actionable steps, you can maintain focus and momentum towards achieving your goals.

Each morning as you ponder question four and reflect on your goals, also scrutinise whether the tasks you've outlined truly contribute to advancing your goals. If a task does not directly align with your objectives, it may be a mandated part of your role. In such cases, consider whether it is imperative to address it immediately or if it can be deferred to a later day. Remember, some tasks may lack significant impact but are necessary nonetheless. By conscientiously evaluating these tasks, you can minimise the depletion of your valuable time.

If you finish your task well within the allocated 60 to 90 minutes, be sure to take a break to recharge. Engage in a brief walk, call a friend, listen to your favourite playlist or treat yourself to something enjoyable. Remember—you do not need to fill the remaining time with other activities. Take a well-deserved break knowing that you've completed a task that moves the needle and impacts your goals.

Once you've completed the high-impact tasks, allocate your remaining time to less critical activities. These might include low-impact, high-urgency tasks or those with low impact and low urgency, such as routine household chores, additional walks for your dog or rearranging furniture. By prioritising tasks that yield the greatest value and impact early on, you'll cultivate a sense of accomplishment and enthusiasm to tackle subsequent responsibilities. Don't forget to carve out time for enjoyment and relaxation. Keep in mind it's not the *quantity* of time spent, but the *quality* of how you utilise it that rejuvenates you.

Also consider your optimal environment for completing high-impact tasks. Will a quiet, distraction-free space foster better focus, or do you thrive in a bustling cafe or outdoor setting for a change of scenery? Exploring different locations can infuse your work with fresh energy, ideas and inspiration.

Additionally, consider incorporating 'walk and talk' meetings into your schedule. These meetings allow you to discuss tasks while moving, providing distance from your usual workspace and laptop. Walking can stimulate creativity and encourage free-flowing conversation, potentially leading to more productive outcomes. By changing up your work settings and methods, you can tap into new sources of motivation and efficiency, ultimately enhancing your overall productivity and joy.

## Summary

Question four of the 5Qs Formula helps you identify three high-impact tasks you choose to focus on each day, which means you get to do more meaningful and purposeful work each day. This approach optimises your productivity by helping you efficiently complete tasks that contribute positively to your goals, rather than merely staying busy with non-value-adding tasks. By prioritising tasks this way, you'll discover that you're essentially accomplishing more with fewer work hours, and achieving greater impact. Remember—ultimately you shape your life and, therefore, own your time. Time is a precious commodity. Utilise it to maximise your impact.

Question four of the 5Qs Formula serves as a powerful tool in guiding your daily time investments. By employing strategies such as the Impact versus Urgency matrix, crafting daily to-do lists focused on three high-impact tasks, implementing time blocking techniques, and confidently saying no to non-value-adding tasks, you can elevate your daily productivity to new heights. This approach leaves you feeling fulfilled, energised and empowered by your accomplishments, and experiencing an overall sense of joy.

# Key takeaways

- Question four of the 5Qs Formula guides you through establishing clear intentions for your daily tasks, which increases your focus, clarity and output.

- Doing impactful things effectively will lead you to experience daily productivity joy.

- Knowing your action or inaction orientation will help you understand what steps you need to take to maximise your productivity and feel energised.

- By identifying specific high-impact tasks for the day, you can effectively allocate your time, attention and energy toward tasks that truly matter to you.

- Question four of the 5Qs Formula allows you to move forward with purpose and clarity without feeling overwhelmed.

- Say goodbye to long daily do-lists; they only cause overwhelm, stress and lack of focus.

- The 'rule of three' is essential to your response to question four of the 5Qs Formula for staying focused, motivated and successful.

- The art of question four of the 5Qs Formula lies in purposeful daily planning that drives action while preventing overthinking, complacency and overwhelm.

- High-impact tasks that make a positive difference are linked to meaningful and purposeful daily living, increasing your motivation, satisfaction and overall joy.

- Valuing your time is an essential component of how you choose to invest it — on what and with whom.

# CHAPTER 7

# Setting your compass

*Question five: How will you show up today?*

Question five is the final component of the 5Qs Formula, yet it holds significant weight. It serves as a helpful compass for your demeanour, presence and daily impact on the world. It creates an intentional choice, a simple and quick decision you make at the start of the day of how you will respond to your day, which will greatly affect how you experience the day.

Through this question, you narrate your day's unfolding, reclaiming agency over your actions and their consequences. Your answer serves as a gateway to clarity, personal responsibility and accountability on how you'll act and behave, as it helps you set the tone and direction of your actions for the day. This question helps you to become clearer on your actions and behaviours. This outward display is driven by intrinsic factors such as your values, strengths, emotions, thoughts and beliefs, addressed by the earlier questions in the 5Qs Formula.

While seemingly straightforward, a thoughtful response to this question empowers you to shape your daily reality, enhance your productivity, and foster feelings of joy, contentment and satisfaction—what I refer to as 'purposeful daily living'.

This chapter will help you learn how to respond to this question in a way that taps into who you are, what is important to you and how you choose to conduct yourself. This will enable you to sculpt your reality regardless of the challenges, hurdles and circumstances you may face each day.

# The power of question five

This question is a powerful tool for you to be the best version of yourself and have a meaningful impact on those around you each day, because it encourages you to be intentional and mindful in your approach to each of your tasks and activities.

For example, this question has helped Mandy with her daily parenting approach. Each day, she reflects and decides that she intends to show up with patience, empathy and positivity. Armed with this intention, she approaches situations differently throughout the day. For instance, when her child spills milk at breakfast, instead of reacting with frustration, Mandy remembers her intention to be patient and responds calmly, helping her child clean up while reassuring her child that accidents happen. Or when her eldest child gets upset over a minor disagreement with a sibling, Mandy recalls her intention to be empathetic, listens attentively to her child's feelings and helps them work through the conflict constructively. By consciously setting her intentions in line with her values, she creates a more positive and nurturing environment for her children and helps herself to be the mother she wants to be. This creates a happy home environment and a happy Mandy.

Another example is Steve, a team leader at a construction firm who also completes the 5Qs Formula each morning. When he responds to question five, he often decides to show up as a supportive, empowering leader who actively listens to his team members' ideas and fosters a culture of collaboration and innovation. He reports that throughout the day, his response to question five influences his actions and interactions with his team. For example, in his morning huddles, instead of dominating the conversation with his own ideas and updates, Steve encourages everyone to share their ideas on an upcoming project. He actively listens to each member, validates their contributions and builds a sense of inclusivity.

Similarly, when Steve conducts feedback sessions with his individual team members, rather than focusing solely on pointing out areas for improvement, Steve approaches each team member's feedback session with empathy and a constructive mindset. He looks to highlight his employee's strengths and offer actionable suggestions for growth. He intentionally fosters a supportive environment for development, which his team notices and appreciates. Steve has started to develop strong trust with his team, and they hold him in high regard and enjoy working with him.

Regardless of your roles in life, age or background, you possess the same chance as anyone else to begin your day intentionally and positively impact yourself and others. It all starts with you!

I learnt this lesson from my youngest son, who at the time was only two and a half years old. He was born in the United Kingdom and exhibited a unique and eccentric personality from a very young age. He had a knack for getting people's attention and engaging with them. Every day, as we walked to his child care in Chiswick, West London, we would pass by a middle-aged homeless man sitting outside the local supermarket, rain or shine. My son, full of energy and cheerfulness, would skip past him and greet him with a warm,

'Morning, have a good day!' in his then British accent. To my initial surprise, the homeless man's face would light up with a beaming smile, and he would return the well wishes, expressing his gratitude for this two year old's kindness. This heartwarming exchange became a regular occurrence, bringing joy to both my son and the homeless man for many months.

One chilly day, the homeless man told me he had something special for my son and had been waiting to give it to him. In all honestly, curiosity mixed with scepticism filled my mind, wondering what a homeless man could offer my son. Nonetheless, we returned the following day, and the man, with a gentle smile, pulled out a large toy fire truck from behind his back. He had been waiting for the right moment to share it with us.

My son looked at the truck, then back at me, seeking permission to accept it. In that moment, my biases and assumptions crept in, questioning the origin and condition of the toy. However, before I could respond, the man began to speak. His voice, though slow and shaky, held a profound sincerity. He explained that this two-year-old boy's presence brightened his day and reminded him of his own children, who were living overseas. He paused, his crooked teeth visible as he sighed deeply, conveying the weight of his emotions.

This interaction demonstrated that regardless of social status, education or economic differences, a simple act of kindness, through the simplest of micro-moments, had made this vulnerable, disadvantaged man feel seen, heard and recognised, and had brought up loving, happy memories for him. Even more than this, it highlights that micro-moments like this don't always need to be planned, intentional or deliberate; they happen when we are willing to show up and be present in the here and now. We gratefully accepted the fire truck, and when we later relocated from London to Melbourne, we took it with us, packed among my son's cherished toys.

This experience opened my eyes to the power of human connection and the capacity each person has to help others experience the love and acceptance each one of us deeply craves. Regardless of age, background or any other differences, we all have a chance each day, in the smallest of moments and interactions, to spread a smile, joy and happiness to all those we interact with when we focus on being intentional and showing up from a place of wanting to make a positive difference.

Bringing this back to the workplace, most adults spend over 70 per cent of their waking day working or thinking about work. Therefore, surely each person is responsible for enabling as many people they interact with or lead to feel a deep sense of belonging, acceptance, and that they matter. This is what I refer to as the true essence of inclusion. You can help this happen in the simplest of micro-moments, and through regular, positive, well-intentioned, meaningful interactions with those you interact with. In this way, people will develop an affinity with you as a colleague, peer, leader or stakeholder, and they will go above and beyond to help you succeed when you show up with good intentions and execute those intentions appropriately.

# Daily values alignment

To choose how you want to show up each day, you need to become clear on your values. These are the principles, beliefs or standards that represent what is important and meaningful to you. They guide your behaviour and decision-making, and how you want to live your life, show up and be remembered. Values are like your moral compass, helping you make decisions and enabling you to choose how, where and with whom you spend and invest your time. They play a fundamental role in shaping your character and identity.

Becoming clear on your values also helps you define what you stand for, and your purpose and being. Although it is easier to live your values when life is going well, it is much harder to live by them when life's daily challenges are testing you. Practising living by your values during good times can make it easier to uphold them during challenging times.

For example, take Katherine, a young professional. Katherine values environmental sustainability, and when everything in her life is going relatively smoothly, she conscientiously recycles, reduces household waste and makes eco-friendly choices without much difficulty. However, her commitment to sustainability is usually compromised when faced with a hectic day filled with deadlines, meetings and unexpected setbacks. On these days, she is tempted to choose convenience over sustainability, such as opting for single-use plastic or driving instead of walking to save time and energy.

Even with the best intentions, facing challenges or setbacks can influence how closely you adhere to your values. Question five doesn't aim to set unrealistic standards or discourage you if you falter in aligning with your intentions and values. Instead, it is a tool to promote accountability for personal growth and encourage you to strive towards becoming the most impactful you. Daily reminders of your values activate your brain, especially the prefrontal cortex responsible for planning, decision-making and goal-directed behaviour. Question five primes you to consider your values and prioritise them in your actions throughout the day.

Remember—even after priming your brain in this manner, it's important to acknowledge that at times things still won't go as planned. You might find yourself behaving in a way that doesn't align with your intentions or feeling less than proud of certain actions. Or perhaps things simply won't pan out as expected. In such cases, you need to be compassionate with yourself.

Recognise what you are doing well and how things could be improved. In this way, you remind yourself you are on a growth journey, continually learning, adjusting and improving. This quality, which I call 'learning agility', is a key skill to develop, because it can help you navigate any situations or circumstances you find yourself in. Always look for growth and improvement, and be able to assess what is and isn't working and change your behaviour, mindset and approach accordingly.

While values are not always easy to live by, they can help you feel aligned, centred, purposeful and connected to what is essential to you. At the same time, when you veer off track like Katherine in the earlier example, your values can serve as a guiding light, directing you back onto the path you truly believe in.

## Expect your values to evolve

Interestingly, while your values are relatively stable over time, they are not set in stone. Instead, your values are prone to change as you progress through various stages of life and evolve as a person. This evolution can manifest in shifts in the importance or priority you assign to different values.

For example, take Zac. In his younger years, Zac prioritised adventure and risk-taking as important values. He used to love travelling and exploring new places. and prioritised those experiences above other aspects of his life. However, Zac's values shifted as he got older and started his family. Like many other parents with young children, he began to prioritise stability, security and family time over the thrill of adventure. Spending quality time with his loved ones and providing a safe and nurturing environment for his family became paramount for him. In this way, Zac's core values of seeking fulfilment and happiness remained consistent; however, the specific values he prioritised evolved to align with his changing circumstances and life experiences.

Change is a natural, inevitable and positive part of life. While people may sometimes say 'you've changed' with a negative connotation, it's important to remember that evolving values isn't a bad thing. Instead, it shows your growth and development. Through experiences, you learn and your values evolve accordingly.

Your brain's neuroplasticity—that is, its ability to reorganise and form new neural connections—enables you to learn and adapt your values over time. As you gain new experiences, develop new insights and receive feedback, you may reassess what matters most to you. This ongoing process can lead to revisions in your values, where certain beliefs or principles become more or less important to you. Additionally, as you navigate through life and encounter different circumstances, your values may shift or become clearer in response to your personal growth or changes in your environment, similar to what happened with Zac.

Therefore, it's worth revisiting the values clarification exercise provided later in this chapter (see the next self-reflection box) at several times in your life to assess where your values are at, and especially when you undergo a significant life change. Common significant life changes for adults include starting a new job or career, moving to a new city or country, graduating from school or university, getting married or moving in with a long-term partner, recovering from a serious illness or injury, buying a house or making a major financial investment, going through a divorce or break-up, having a child or becoming a parent, retiring from work or starting a new phase of life, or experiencing the loss of a loved one.

# The importance of values alignment

Psychological research indicates that when your values align with your external environment (whether that's your workplace, relationships, place of education or social groups), you tend to experience greater wellbeing and satisfaction in your job, studies or social interactions and overall life. This alignment enhances your productivity since your attention and focus can more easily engage with your tasks, rather than being diverted by conflicts in values. Psychologists refer to this alignment as 'values congruency'—that is, a congruency between your personal values and the context in which you operate or spend most of your time. When this congruency is in place, you will experience higher levels of harmony, fulfilment and capacity to focus on completing what's important to you.

Imagine working in an environment where you can see a clear disconnect between the leadership's decision-making processes and how they treat their staff. Let's consider Danny, a leader at an emerging technology start-up. Danny has a habit of shouting at his staff when he's dissatisfied with their work or ideas, even going as far as to scream down the phone at them. Vivian, another leadership team member, finds Danny's behaviour deeply troubling. It contradicts her fundamental values of what constitutes great leadership.

Danny's behaviour remains unchanged, despite Vivian having conversations with him and offering suggestions on how he could approach situations differently with his staff. Vivian feels increasingly uncomfortable and conflicted with each interaction with Danny and each day she's at work. Much of her time and attention goes into 'damage control', supporting the staff and trying to lift their dampened morale and confidence, which limits her own productivity levels. Ultimately, Vivian makes the difficult yet courageous decision to leave the organisation.

During her exit interview with the new human resources lead, Vivian cites the misalignment between her values and those demonstrated by the leadership team, and particularly Danny's behaviour, as the primary reason for her departure. This example illustrates the ripple effect of conflicting values between leadership and employees on a workplace's culture and employee retention, as well as its ability to attract new employees. People are more likely to share and remember negative news and stories they hear or experience; therefore, such leadership as Danny's, will likely harm the company's brand, affecting future growth and the leader's reputation.

When you make decisions or engage in behaviours that align with your values, even if such decisions or actions are challenging, your brain's reward system becomes activated. This activation involves the release of dopamine, generating positive feelings and serving as a form of positive reinforcement for your commitment and adherence to your values. For example, if you highly value honesty and choose to tell the truth in a difficult situation, even when it might have negative consequences—for example, admitting a mistake—your brain's reward system is likely to release dopamine. This dopamine release will make you feel good about your decision to uphold your value of honesty, reinforcing your commitment to that value in the future.

I vividly recall a moment of unexpected joy shared with a stranger in London. It began with the frantic realisation that I had left my purse on a bustling city bus during a routine trip back from Chiswick to Kew Gardens, holding my youngest in his baby carrier on my chest, and squeezing the hand of my eldest. We watched in despair as the bus continued on its way, with my purse still on the seat we'd just left. Panic set in as I grasped the gravity of the situation—my wallet, bank cards, ear pods, £50 note and a sentimental keychain, all lost in a moment of frenzy.

On returning home, I contacted the necessary authorities and scoured for any glimmer of hope. My eldest son, wise beyond his years at just five, brought me a smile of hope: 'You never know, Mumma. There are good people in this world'.

Weeks passed with no sign of my lost belongings until, lying awake at night, a thought crossed my mind. My purse had my driver's license in it, which had my previous address listed on it. In the morning, I contacted my previous neighbour and told her what had happened. She graciously inquired with the new occupants and, remarkably, a conscientious man had left notes for the new occupants, indicating he had found something valuable on the bus. They forwarded the diligent man's number to me and I promptly contacted him, his words simple and his voice thick with a Nigerian accent. He asked me a series of questions to verify my identity and the contents of the purse. Once satisfied that the purse belonged to me, he agreed to meet me at a local supermarket the next day to return it. I couldn't help but wonder if this could truly be happening.

In anticipation and hope, I decided to express my gratitude by bringing along a box of deluxe chocolates and a bottle of wine. The following day, his face lit up with an overjoyed smile when I met him and he handed me the purse. Overwhelmed with gratitude, I sought to repay his honourable kindness, but he humbly declined, expressing that his greatest reward was doing the right thing.

As I opened the purse, I was amazed to find everything still inside, including the £50. Completely moved by his selflessness, I asked if we could take a photograph together. I wanted to not only express my gratitude to him, but also show my son, to reinforce his belief in the inherent goodness of humanity. I was truly left in awe of this man's dedication to doing the right thing and how all his actions embodied integrity. He could have taken many other actions, but these were not in line with his values.

# Self-reflection

What are your core values? Most people think they know their values, but when you ask them to be specific, they need help. Also, some of your values may be based on what you remember your parents believing, your upbringing or cultural norms. They may not accurately reflect who you are today, what you aspire to be or what you consider of higher importance to your current phase in life. This exercise will help you identify which values are most important to you now, during your current phase of your life, and help you determine your top five values.

For this exercise, I've provided a list of typical values, and my version of their unique definitions, in the appendix. You will need to spend approximately 20 minutes in a quiet space reading through the list.

## Step one

Read through each value statement in the appendix and give each a rating that most closely reflects what the value means to you. The ratings are as follows:

- *Deal-breaker:* This value is of super importance to you, and if you or someone crosses this value, it is a show-stopper for you!

- *So/so:* This value isn't of the highest importance to you — it's a little bit like a 'nice to have'. You agree with it, but it's not quite a deal breaker.

- *Nah:* This value is not necessary or as important to you.

Insert a 'D', 'S' or 'N' next to each value. Don't think about your assessment too much. It's best to go with your gut feeling, because this is normally your most instinctual and, therefore, most authentic response.

## Step two

Go through the complete list of values again, revisiting the ones you've rated as a 'Deal-breaker' or 'So/so'. Ask yourself which are of the most important to you.

The aim of this exercise is to end up with only five values that are most important to you as deal-breakers. You may need to review your 'Deal-breaker' and 'So/so' choices several times to eliminate values or consider which ones are most important.

## Step three

Once you have your five deal-breaker values, write them down in a place where you will see them each day. You might want to write them on a sticky note and put them on your fridge or your bathroom mirror. This way, you can see them each morning and night when you open your fridge or brush your teeth.

Ensure you are clear on what each of your five values means to you. To help with this, either use the definition provided or tweak its description so the value is directly relevant to you.

For example, say you chose 'curiosity' as one of your five most important values. According to my definition, 'curiosity' means to be open-minded, inquisitive and ready to discover. A tweaked definition of this value for you might be always being open-minded and open-hearted, willing to discover something new and perhaps let go of something old.

As another example, perhaps you picked 'courage' as an important value. My definition is to tap into my inner strength, even when it scares me to do so. A tweaked definition of this value for you might be to play *big*, not small, and be fearless. When I think big, my problems seem small!

*(continued)*

Courage is asking myself the question, 'What one thing will I do today that will push me out of my comfort zone?' Only when you push past your fears, when you stop worrying about making a fool of yourself and stop caring what others think of you, will you truly live and love your life!

As evident from the two examples just provided, refining the definitions for the values you've chosen is important. The more relevant and meaningful the values are to you, the more deeply they will resonate with you. And the more you can relate to your chosen values, the more likely you are to identify with them, embody them and take pride in what they mean to you.

## Step four

Once you have your five values, take a moment to reflect and ask yourself whether any of your chosen values surprise you. Had you expected other specific values to be in your top five, and they are not?

This small check-in is an excellent way to see if your values have changed since you last considered them, or if you have confirmed what you thought they were all along.

You will get considerable value (pardon the pun) from the preceding self-reflection exercise, because values play a significant role in shaping your thoughts, identity and self-concept. Your five identified values will influence how you perceive yourself and your role in the world. You will experience an alignment between your head, heart and gut, leading to greater levels of wellbeing and overall fulfilment, when you live true to your values.

For example, if you highly value kindness, you will likely perceive yourself as a compassionate person who prioritises acts of kindness. This value may also influence how you spend your time, such as volunteering or doing pro-bono work. Helping those in need would further reinforce your self-identity as someone who values kindness.

James Clear summarised this eloquently with these words (quoted in chapter 1 but also worth repeating here): 'Every action you take is a vote for the type of person you wish to become'.

## Values determine who you spend time with

Due to the similarity and familiarity bias, you are also likely to be attracted to others who share similar values. Psychological studies have found that couples with similar values report higher levels of relationship satisfaction and stay together longer. Similarly, studies have shown that friendships are more likely to form and be maintained when individuals have similar values and interests.

When your beliefs and actions are in harmony with your values, it frees up mental energy for important, high-impact tasks, increasing daily productivity. Additionally, living in line with your values promotes a sense of fulfilment and happiness, contributing to overall positive wellbeing and energy levels.

Social psychologist Leon Festinger developed the cognitive consistency theory in the 1950s, which suggests you are motivated to maintain cognitive harmony by seeking relationships with others who share your values. Doing so helps reduce cognitive dissonance, which is the discomfort experienced when a mismatch exists between your beliefs and your actions, or between different beliefs.

For example, let's say you highly value health and fitness, and you prioritise exercising regularly and eating nutritious foods. However, your best friend consistently engages in unhealthy behaviours such as consuming fast food regularly and rarely exercising. This situation creates a cognitive dissonance for you because of the mismatch between your belief in health and fitness and your best friend's behaviour.

To reduce the discomfort, you might encourage your best friend to adopt healthier habits, aligning their actions more closely with your values. Or you may rationalise the inconsistency by telling yourself that your best friend's behaviour is their choice and doesn't affect your health choices. Seeking out friendships with others who prioritise health and fitness in the same way you do can help reduce the cognitive dissonance and reinforce the importance of this value for you.

Interacting with others who share your values promotes cognitive harmony within you and, again, frees up mental energy for important, high-impact tasks, increasing your daily productivity.

An example of connecting with people authentically and being guided by your shared values comes from my speaking experience. When my family and I migrated back to Melbourne from London in 2021, in the middle of the global pandemic, I was eager to build my business and brand in the Australian corporate world. Developing trusted relationships takes time and I find that in-person meetings foster connection and trust more quickly. So, I was thrilled to be invited to present a keynote on 'Joy of Work' to an auditorium full of HR leaders and C-Suite executives at a leadership conference in Melbourne. This was my first in-person engagement in my new home since the pandemic, and I felt both nervous and excited.

After a fabulous introduction by the MC, I walked onto the stage, took a deep breath, grounded myself and smiled. I quietly said to myself 'I am safe'—a proven and very effective strategy to help you overcome your nerves before any type of speaking gig. Those simple words provide reassurance to your brain, calming your emotions and centring your thinking. I remember looking out at the audience and acknowledging the beauty of being together in person after months of lockdown. I delivered the keynote and was very humbly pleased to receive a roar of claps and joyous cheers. One HR leader approached me privately afterwards and shared that while listening to the talk, she had gone to my website and scheduled a meeting for the following Monday.

The following Monday, I had a virtual meeting with the HR leader, and we discussed a programme for 90 of her leaders. I asked questions to understand her needs and her definition of success for the team, participants and organisation. To my surprise, within a week, the program was signed off and I delivered it to 90 leaders across 20 countries. Curious, I asked the HR leader what convinced her to work with me. I expected her to mention the research and psychological science I shared. Instead, she said it was my personal stories, my vulnerability and relatability, that made her want her leaders to experience my approach.

I share this story because it reinforced my learnings that people do business with people they know, like and trust. It's crucial to get strong at building connection by knowing your values, being authentic and connecting with others simultaneously on two levels—emotionally and logically.

## Not connecting with your values sets you up to fail

When your actions are not aligned with how you want to show up each day, you are likely to encounter challenges that undermine the impact you truly desire. For instance, you may feel dissatisfied or unfilled in your personal or professional life, struggle to maintain meaningful relationships or connect with others, experience inner conflict, and/or face difficulties in achieving or making progress on goals and decisions. All of these challenges lead to increased stress, anxiety, burnout, loss of motivation or purpose, and reduced productivity and overall wellbeing. Similarly, ignoring or going against your values will usually result in feelings of guilt, inner conflict and dissatisfaction.

An example of this is Manoj, a senior leader at a local council who values kindness and empathy. He makes an effort to greet his co-workers warmly each time he's working from the office, because he's very conscious of creating a positive atmosphere in the workplace. However, on a particularly stressful day Manoj arrives at the office feeling frazzled and preoccupied. He inadvertently snaps at a colleague who asks for his help. This reaction impacts his relationship with this co-worker and disrupts the positive and supportive environment he has been trying to create.

Without intentionally priming his mind at the start of the day to connect with his values of kindness and empathy, a moment of heightened stress and preoccupation led him to behave in a way that undermined the impact he wanted to have. Manoj felt upset with himself and later apologised to his colleague.

This is why question five intentionally prompts you to think about your values and consider which of your five values you will lean into each day to help you achieve what you need and want to do in the best way possible. Doing so optimises your productivity, reducing unnecessary friction along the way and helping you stay aligned with your authentic self, enabling you to achieve your goals more effectively.

## Show up by playing to your strengths

When responding to question five, considering which strengths you want to tap into for the day is also helpful. Did you know everyone has a unique set of strengths? You, too, have your own superpowers that come naturally to you, and when you use them, you feel energised and accomplished. Strengths consist of two key components: things you are good at and activities you enjoy. When you use your strengths to complete tasks, it feels effortless; you become fully absorbed in what you're doing and feel happy. Psychologist Mihaly Csikszentmihalyi eloquently defined this experience as being in 'flow' in his book *Flow: The Psychology of Optimal Experience*. He describes 'flow' as a state of complete absorption and focus in an activity, where your skills and strengths align with the challenge. In this state of flow, you often lose track of time and feel a deep sense of satisfaction and fulfilment.

For over 60 years, researchers have considered strengths-based psychology, popularised by psychologist Donald O Clifton. (Clifton went on to develop the StrengthsFinder assessment, now known as the CliftonStrengths assessment owned by Gallup.) Among other findings, this research has shown that when you use your strengths in your daily life, you are three times more likely to report having an excellent quality of life.

Playing to your strengths helps you deliver your tasks more effectively and quickly. For example, if one of your strengths is 'organising', reminding yourself of this strength will help you plan a complex project that otherwise may feel daunting or overwhelming. Or if one of your strengths is 'problem-solving', reminding yourself of this strength can assist you in navigating unexpected challenges or obstacles that arrive during a project. When faced with a difficult decision or issue, leveraging your problem-solving strength will enable you to develop various new ideas or solutions to help the project progress. Applying your strengths to daily activities and tasks will optimise your effectiveness, productivity and spark.

# Self-reflection

This exercise helps you identify your superpowers. Give yourself 30 minutes to complete it, and find somewhere without distraction.

## Step one

Draw a table (or create one on your device) with three columns. In the first column, write down all the tasks and activities you get to do on a typical day that you are good at — perhaps you know you are good at this task or activity, you receive praise from others in this area, or the outcomes show it.

## Step two

In the second column of your table, write down all the tasks and activities you enjoy doing. Immersing yourself in these tasks or activities brings you joy and energy, and you can lose track of time.

## Step three

Where you see a duplication of the same activity or task in both columns, highlight them in the same colour — completing these kinds of activities or tasks is likely to be one of your strengths or superpowers. Now come up with a label that reflects that strength or superpower. The following table provides some examples.

**Finding your strengths**

| Tasks *good* at | Tasks *enjoyed* | Your label for the strength |
|---|---|---|
| Analysing data | | |
| Coming up with ideas | Coming up with ideas | Innovator |
| Organising events | | |
| Getting people on side | Getting people on side | Influencer |
| Meeting deadlines | Meeting deadlines | Reliable |
| Researching information | Researching information | Researcher |

Remember that a strength is defined by two things: what you are good at *and* what you enjoy. You may find you have many or very few duplications across both columns. Try to keep going until you reach at least five duplications across the two columns, because most people will likely have at least five key strengths.

If you struggle with this exercise — perhaps you can't identify five duplications between the first and second columns or are undecided about your top five strengths — it may be because you don't have a consistent language to describe your strengths. Various strengths assessment tests are available online, some of which are free. However, I recommend the CliftonStrengths Assessment. Go to www.gallup.com/cliftonstrengths for more information and to purchase the assessment. After responding to the assessment questions, you will receive a report that highlights your top five strengths, from the 34 strengths available in the psychometric.

# Counteracting negative thoughts

Question five also serves as a useful tool for redirecting your mindset when faced with unhelpful or negative thoughts about yourself at the start of the day. By contemplating how you intend to show up, you can shift your focus away from any self-doubt or criticism and instead establish a positive, constructive intention for the day.

For example, if you're grappling with feelings of inadequacy and thoughts that you are not good enough, you can intentionally choose to approach the day by being bold, confident and self-assured. Sometimes, it only takes a simple reminder to yourself that you are capable at the start of the day to reset your mindset. Similarly, you can remind yourself of the things you have already achieved, or the challenges you have faced in the past. Remember—your brain is likely to forget all the amazing stuff you have done due to its negativity bias, as discussed in chapters 4 and 5. In this way, question five helps counteract any negative thoughts about yourself at the beginning of the day, setting you up for a positive, effective and enjoyable day.

Creating what I like to call a 'victory vault' can also be incredibly helpful. This document serves as a record of your achievements and the things you're most proud of. By keeping your victory vault in an accessible and visible place, you can easily remind yourself of your accomplishments, especially when you feel doubtful or low in confidence. This acts to prime your brain to recall all that you have been able to achieve before, encouraging you to keep pushing forward and reinforcing your belief that you've got this!

# Domino effect of how you show up

As humans, we are inherently drawn to human connection. Even if you reside alone, you don't truly live in isolation, devoid of any form of human interaction, unless you inhabit a remote island, cave or desert. How you conduct yourself—your demeanour, attitude and actions—has a ripple effect on others. Being mindful and intentional about how you show up can influence others to have positive experiences, interactions and moments of growth and learning of their own when with you.

In contrast, when you show up preoccupied or self-serving, others may feel disconnected or undervalued in your presence. Your demeanour and actions significantly shape how others perceive you and whether they metaphorically choose to move closer to you or choose to distance themselves from you. By radiating optimism, demonstrating a commitment to serving others and creating space for them to be themselves, you can help others feel seen, heard, valued and appreciated. Ultimately, everyone wants to feel like they matter and I believe we all have a personal responsibility to help those around us experience this.

As a result, you will find people will enjoy your company and that both you and they will experience personal growth, fulfilment and satisfaction in the time shared together. Ultimately, you have the power to decide the type of role model you want to be and the legacy you wish to leave behind, whether this is in fleeting encounters or in lasting relationships.

Question five gives you the opportunity to take personal responsibility for how you will show up and the impact you want to have on those around you each day. If we all took the time to intentionally choose how we will show up and respond to others, the world would be a calmer, kinder and happier place. My thinking on this aligns closely with the Arbinger Institute's approach to mindset, which emphasises personal responsibility and adopting an outward mindset rather than an inward mindset.

An outward mindset involves taking responsibility for your actions and their impact on others. People with an outward mindset are more empathetic, understanding and collaborative, recognising that others also have their own needs, objectives and challenges. In contrast, those with an inward mindset focus primarily on their own objectives, needs and perspectives, often leading to self-justification, blame and a lack of accountability for the impact of their actions on others.

Question five of the 5Qs Formula helps you actively shift from an inward to an outward mindset. It encourages you to take accountability for how you show up in various situations, and make conscious choices to act in ways that are supportive and considerate of others.

This understanding of personal responsibility and mindset is further supported by psychologist Susan Fiske's research, known as the 'stereotype content model', which reveals how humans tend to associate qualities such as warmth and friendliness with competence and ability. For example, when someone appears warm and friendly—that is, they display a more outward mindset—you are more likely to assume they possess other positive qualities such as skills, intelligence and ability.

So, if you want to genuinely win others over through your daily interactions, show up in a manner that is authentic, sincere and warm. In this way, others will also perceive you as capable and knowledgeable. By developing your emotional intelligence, you can learn to express your warmth through more ways than just what you say or do. For example, you can express warmth through social cues such as your body language, tone of voice and facial expressions, all of which are visible to others as they try to get to know you. By being mindful and intentional about how you show up, you can have a more significant positive impact on those around you, and they, too, will be drawn closer to you in the process. Back in 1971, church leader Carl W Buehner expressed this wonderfully: 'They may forget what you said—but they will never forget how you made them feel'. (A similarly worded quote is often misattributed to Maya Angelou.) This idea links back to question one in chapter 3, in that people will be drawn to your emotional energy, because humans are all fundamentally dynamic beings with interconnected emotions and energies. People will sense your energy even before you utter a word!

When you show up with intentionality and authenticity, in alignment with your values while leveraging your strengths, you cultivate trust with others. In this state, you'll feel at ease and make a meaningful impact simply by being yourself, without pretending to be someone else. It's essential to remember that nobody else can embody your unique essence better than you. With everyone else already spoken for, you can embrace and cultivate your unique identity, tailor-made just for you. No-one else can do you better than you!

# Applying the 5Qs Formula: Question five

Question five has been deliberately placed as the final step in the 5Qs Formula, following the identification of the three high-impact tasks you aim to accomplish in a given day. This strategic positioning is intended to emphasise the significance of understanding what you need to achieve, and how you must approach your day from a mindset and behavioural perspective to accomplish those tasks successfully. Remember—you're not aiming to simply tick items off a list; you want to execute them in a manner that aligns with your values, leverages your strengths, fosters a helpful mindset and brings you joy. Answering this question ensures you are prepared and motivated to tackle the day's challenges, and increases your chances of feeling satisfied with how you conducted yourself through the day.

To respond effectively to question five, first complete the values clarification exercise from earlier in this chapter, so you have your top five values captured somewhere easily accessible, such as in your journal and on a place visible in your home or workplace. Secondly, complete the strengths reflection exercise so you are clear on your top five strengths. Also capture these in your journal and keep them in a place visible in your home or workplace.

Each morning, as you complete the 5Qs Formula and reach question five, refer to your top five values list and your top five strengths. Identify which two to three values and/or one to two strengths you will lean into and focus on that day. Write them down in your journal, expressing your commitment to them. Since these are the last things you will capture as part of your 5Qs Formula, you are most likely to remember them, thanks to your brain's recency effect, which means your brain prioritises the first and last parts of the 5Qs Formula.

For example, Jacqueline is a team leader at a telecommunications firm. As she completes the 5Qs Formula in the morning, she knows she has a difficult conversation with a team member that day. She has noticed a drop in the team member's performance, and suspects this is due to an underlying issue. Jacqueline is also concerned about an important looming client deadline, which this team member is responsible for meeting. In response to question five of the 5Qs Formula, Jacqueline recognises the need for a tough conversation and reminds herself of her values of respecting and supporting others. She also acknowledges the benefit of leaning into her strengths of communication and problem-solving. She knows she will need to show up in a way which makes the team member feel heard, respected and supported. She also knows she will need to listen to the team member's concerns, offer guidance, and jointly develop a plan for improvement and alternative resources to meet the deadline. In this way, Jacqueline decides she will schedule in a private meeting with the team member to discuss their challenges openly and constructively. Jacqueline's intentions demonstrate her commitment to the wellbeing and development of her team member, as well as fostering a positive and productive work environment.

Or take Amaya, a mother of three children. She knows she has a busy Saturday doing parent duties, including taking her children to different activities—one has an important exam while another has a concert practice—and dealing with her third child, who is going through a phase of being difficult and stroppy with anyone and everything. When Amaya responds to question five on this particular day, she reminds herself of her values of being positive and being calm, and her strength of planning. She acknowledges that the day won't be easy, but she intends to remain calm, composed and positive, despite how her children behave. In this way, she speaks calmly, repeats her instructions clearly to her children, and also acknowledges and praises any positive behaviours she notices to encourage and show them she is working with each of them. She also shares with them that she's doing her best and needs them to work with her. While she was able to take the children on time to their activities, she was also able to remain calm and composed, despite the younger child's difficult, whining behaviour, and even as it persists through to the end of the day. Amaya felt exhausted at the end of the day, but when she reflected, she was overall pleased with how she handled herself and the children (despite a few 'oh my god!' moments).

Amaya's situation reflects the South African philosophy of Ubuntu, which translates to 'I am because we are'. This philosophy underscores the interconnectedness of individuals and communities, emphasising that how you show up and your actions affect others. In Amaya's busy day, her commitment to remaining positive, calm and composed despite the challenges of her day demonstrates the Ubuntu principles. By acknowledging her values of positivity and composure, and drawing on her strength of planning, Amaya not only navigates her day effectively but also fosters a supportive environment for her children. Through her actions, Amaya demonstrates compassion, empathy and mutual respect, creating a space where everyone's wellbeing is valued.

Also consider Miguel, who's been preoccupied with an impending client presentation scheduled for today. This has already been postponed and rescheduled twice by the client. Feeling nervous about the presentation, Miguel also finds himself somewhat frustrated with the client for the prolonged delays. When he, too, completes question five, he recalls his values of gratitude and forgiveness. This mental exercise helps him to shift his mindset, and approach the presentation with a sense of thankfulness for the opportunity and openness to consider other demands placed on the client. In doing so, he redirects the energy that would have been consumed by his initial negativity for the client, towards a more productive and positive outlook. This shift in both perspective and energy allows him to show up with confidence, compassion and humility, thereby ensuring a positive client experience.

Finally, let's take Jasmine. She has a family function this evening that she has not been looking forward to—she finds her aunts and uncles are always questioning how she spends her time and why she hasn't got a clear plan of what she wants to do with her life. She knows she's unable to avoid going to the function and, therefore, decides as she completes question five that she is going to show up with her values of fun, honesty and self-awareness. In this way, Jasmine chooses to approach the function with a different mindset. Instead of feeling defensive or annoyed by her relatives' inquiries, she reframes their curiosity as reflecting their concern and interest in her wellbeing. Embracing her values, she decides to inject some playfulness into the conversations, acknowledging their caring intentions while gently reminding them that it's okay not to have everything figured out. Jasmine also decides to take the initiative to steer conversations towards more positive and meaningful topics. In this way, Jasmine is likely to transform her own experience of the family function and also leave a lasting, nuanced yet positive impression on her family members.

Sometimes, situations may arise where relying solely on your top values or strengths may not be the most effective approach. In such cases, other values or strengths not in your top five may be better suited to helping you navigate a situation effectively. Asking yourself question five can help you consider alternative approaches and determine how to best show up in the situation, even if it means drawing on values or strengths that are not your primary focus but are still of some importance to you.

Bobby experienced just this when planning a surprise 40th birthday party for his partner, Puja. He wanted everything to be perfect. While his top strengths revolved around organisation and meticulous attention to detail, however, he also understood that what was truly needed to create an unforgettable party was creativity and spontaneity. Question five prompted Bobby to broaden his perspective and lean into qualities such as creativity and flexibility.

Instead of solely relying on his strengths in planning and structure, Bobby embraced the opportunity to infuse the party with imaginative touches and unexpected surprises. By incorporating elements of spontaneity and creative flair, Bobby succeeded in making the party truly memorable and enjoyable for Puja. He achieved this by being adaptable and willing to go beyond his usual strengths and lean into some discomfort.

In a similar scenario, manager Taylor needed to provide constructive feedback to a direct report who had consistently missed deadlines. While Taylor's top strengths lay in strategic thinking and analytical skills, she recognised the importance of delivering feedback with empathy and emotional intelligence. Despite these not being her primary strengths, question five prompted Taylor to approach the feedback conversation with sensitivity and understanding.

Taylor dedicated time to prepare for the discussion, ensuring she had specific examples of missed deadlines and their impact. During the meeting, she actively listened to her direct report's perspective, acknowledging their challenges and offering support. By leveraging alternative strengths in empathy and communication, Taylor delivered the feedback constructively, focusing on co-creating solutions and exploring actionable steps for improvement.

Once you are familiar with your values and strengths, and are willing to lean into other values and strengths when needed, responding to question five daily will become easier and simpler. Over time, you may also find your responses to this question becoming consistent or similar. This is beneficial because it reinforces what is important to you and allows you to navigate various situations effectively. Intentionally leaning into your values and strengths will become more habitual as you continue this practice. Keeping this practice going is essential to keep your values and strengths top of mind, especially as life and the demands placed on you get more complex and busier. Question five provides your guardrails, akin to those in bowling lanes, preventing you from veering off course, stumbling or losing your way and instead helping to keep you on course.

## Summary

Question five prompts you to set a positive intention for your day, which will help you focus on behaviours, thoughts and feelings that align with your values and goals. In this way, you foster a sense of authenticity and integrity in your day. This question also encourages ownership of your attitude and approach to the day. It reminds you that you can choose how you respond to situations and interact with others. It prompts you to connect with your values and strengths daily, leaving you feeling accomplished, satisfied and fulfilled.

# Key takeaways

- Question five prompts you to make an intentional choice at the start of the day of how you will respond to your day.

- This powerful question also prompts you to make a meaningful daily impact, and experience purposeful daily living.

- Regardless of your roles in life, you have the same chance as anyone else to start your day with intention and positivity.

- Your values act as a moral compass, providing guidelines and principles for how you want to live your life, how you want to show up and be remembered.

- Sticking to your values is easier when things are going well and harder when things are challenging, but not impossible.

- Your values will determine who you spend time with.

- Strengths are made up of things: what you are good at *and* what you enjoy doing.

- Knowing your strengths allows you to lean into them more, which leaves you feeling productive, satisfied and energised.

- By staying true to your values and leveraging your strengths, you create a ripple effect of positivity that influences those around you. This shapes the legacy you wish to leave and ensures you are remembered for the impact you make in the lives of others.

- Living each day in line with your strengths and values enables you to achieve more of what matters and brings you joy.

# PART III

# Additional aspects to consider

# CHAPTER 8

# Your oxygen mask

Remember the most recent flight you took. As the flight attendant went through the safety procedures, one of the first instructions given to you and all the other passengers was to put your oxygen mask on first in an emergency. You are clearly reminded that in the event of a sudden loss of cabin pressure, you should secure your own oxygen mask before assisting others, including your children or those needing help. This instructional advice teaches us an important life skill: your ability to assist others effectively is only achieved by first ensuring your own safety and wellbeing.

This chapter is all about helping you secure your own oxygen mask first, not just in an emergency but as part of your regular practice to thrive. Self-care is not a luxury; it's a necessity and must be part of your daily approach to thriving.

You cannot be an optimal and impactful version of yourself by running dry on a low-energy tank or barely scraping by. Looking after yourself is essential to your daily productivity and joy. By regularly having your oxygen mask on, you will fuel your body, brain and spirit with an attractive energy that can enable you to conquer all you set out to do, with purpose, meaning and impact.

The 5Qs Formula sets your mind, focus and attention up for daily success in terms of productivity, fulfilment and joy. In addition to the 5Qs Formula, taking care of your overall wellbeing, including physical, spiritual and social wellbeing, is essential. This chapter helps you focus on incorporating additional tools to add to your daily toolkit, which will help you achieve holistic wellbeing and truly help you become the most impactful version of yourself.

My lifelong mission has been to empower as many people as possible to become the most impactful versions of themselves because, in this way, they live well, and so does everyone around them. The ripple effect each of us can have on those around us is incredible. When we realise this, each one of us can start to take responsibility to play a role in optimising ourselves and, in turn, uplifting those around us. They go on to uplift those around them, and collectively, we advance humanity and positively impact the world for generations to follow.

# The power of your oxygen mask

Taking care of your wellbeing by putting on your own oxygen mask first can be broken down into the following areas:

- sleep

- movement

- nutrition

- calm

- connection

- learning.

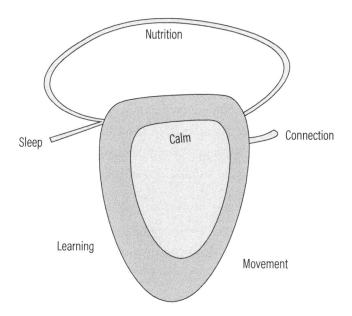

**The power of your oxygen mask**

## *The power of quality sleep*

How is your sleep? Do you get quality sleep? Do you wake up in the morning feeling refreshed? Or do you wake up feeling tired, foggy-headed and groggy? Would you love to wake up feeling alert and ready for the day?

It can seem like one of the worst feelings when you struggle to fall asleep at night, or wake in the morning after broken or uninterrupted sleep. A lack of sleep can make you feel worn out, irritable, frustrated and drained. I remember (not so fondly) the sleepless nights and interrupted nights of sleep I had while my boys were young. I went to sleep school—not once, but twice—while living in Australia with my firstborn. This is a fabulous service offered in Australia for parents, where the mother goes to stay for a week with her baby and, throughout the day and night, receives support and help in learning and practising sleeping techniques to get the baby into a sleep and feeding routine that also provides somewhat of a respite for the mother. My husband would join us in the evenings and we would have dinner together. When we arrived home from sleep school and were all home together, my husband and I worked out a shared care arrangement to take those night sleeps in turns, which helped tremendously. Unfortunately, the sleep school service was not offered in the United Kingdom where I had my second child. We went through many interrupted nights of sleep with him while trying to hold down our demanding jobs and take care of our eldest son.

When you are busy, have lots on your mind and know you have lots to do, switching your mind off and going to sleep can be challenging. You are not a robot with an on-and-off switch. (Sometimes, I wish that could be an option.)

You win the day by winning the night before. What do I mean by this? You need to have a good sleep routine in place to ensure you sleep well, and wake up ready to start the day intentionally and with impact.

When well-rested, you can take on the day's challenges and interactions with others. Your attention is more likely to be centred and focused rather than scattered, irritable, distracted, or not fully present and engaged. 'Winning the night before' involves thinking about your evening routine, prioritising the key things that need to be done, and identifying the things that can be switched to another day, delegated, or dropped.

In this way, you prioritise the essential tasks—for example, having dinner, getting the children to sleep, doing your exercise or house chores, preparing anything you need for the next day and, hopefully, enjoying some downtime, where you can relax and unwind. Remember to focus on the *quality* of time you spend in downtime rather than the *quantity*. For example, you may only have 15 or 20 minutes to unwind, so you may decide to read a book, listen to your favourite podcast or watch a part of an episode of your favourite show. Having this discipline to focus on quality versus quantity means you can help your brain and body feel the benefits of the downtime without feeling disheartened that it wasn't enough time.

A good sleep routine means you get to bed at a particular time each night, and allow yourself seven to eight hours of sleep, where possible. Everyone is different and likely to have individualised requirements and circumstances. You may need slightly more hours of sleep or fewer. Regardless of the time you wake up, it's crucial to establish a routine to go to bed at a specific time. For example, whenever possible, I try to be in bed by 9.30 pm to wake up by 5.15 am. This routine did not come naturally to me, but I developed it over time and worked on implementing it consistently so I could optimise myself. Your timings may be different and this is fine too. The key is to put in place times that work for you to help you optimise.

Think about your evening routine. Could you change, delegate or even drop something to help ensure you get to sleep and have at least seven to eight hours of quality sleep per night?

During my counselling days and running my first business, Minds For The Future, which I sold in 2015, I found many of my clients suffered from poor-quality sleep due to overthinking, overwhelm and busy lifestyles. I used my knowledge of psychological research and expertise to develop a relaxation technique to help improve their quality of sleep. I called this relaxation technique the Three Anchors, and it helped hundreds of my clients get to sleep quicker and enjoy quality sleep throughout the night.

The Three Anchors technique helps calm your mind and body and brings your brain wave activity to the alpha state. It involves three key steps: breathing, relaxing your limbs, and activating your senses. When your brain wave activity is in the alpha state you are calm, relaxed and balanced. The Three Anchors relaxation technique is grounded in psychological science and can be applied by anyone, regardless of age, background or occupation. You can download your complimentary copy of this unique Three Anchors guided relaxation exercise from simirayat.com or by scanning the QR code at the end of the book.

Here are three super practical steps to help you experience better-quality sleep, incorporating the Three Anchors relaxation technique:

1. *Set a consistent bedtime and stick to it:* As much as possible, ensure you are always in bed at the time you set. This may mean adjusting your routine or reassessing all the things you need to do before the end of the day. You may like to watch TV or scroll social media to unwind. While this is fine, try to ensure you have the discipline to stick with your sleep time. Of course, always sticking to your established bedtime can be tricky, especially if you have young children or other caring responsibilities or fancy a late night out. However, sticking to it wherever possible will help you ensure you get good-quality sleep. You may wish to stick to a consistent bedtime during the weekdays and be more flexible with your sleep times during the weekends.

2. *Put your phone away:* Leave your phone in a different room at night so you are less likely to be distracted by aimless scrolling just before sleep or when you wake first thing in the morning. Your brain is the most vulnerable to being shaped and influenced when you first wake up, and by not having your phone easily accessible, you can prevent yourself from being influenced by whatever comes up on your scroll or feed. If, like myself, you are used to using your phone as your alarm clock, buy yourself an old-school digital alarm clock so you can leave your phone out of reach. Empower

yourself in the morning by applying the 5Qs Formula, which will set you up to be the best version of you for the day ahead and will positively shape your brain!

3. *Apply the Three Anchors relaxation technique:* Use this eight-minute relaxation exercise when you get into bed before you fall asleep. This technique helps you calm your mind, relax your body and prime your brain to focus on joy and smiles. In turn, this helps you sleep peacefully and get the rest you deserve to conquer the next day in the best way possible.

# The power of moving

In life's intricate dance, movement isn't just an option; it's the very essence of your growth and vitality. Whether it's a leisurely stroll or a sweat-inducing gym class, each step forward speaks volumes about your dedication to evolve. After years of dragging my feet, and making lots of excuses and prioritising other things, I started to experience the transformative addiction of early-morning exercise workouts.

Through committing to 6 am grind sessions—from intense HIIT workouts to fast-paced cycling classes, and core-focused reformer Pilates to comprehensive muscle strength training—I was able to make changes to my physical body and, even more so, to my mental strength. In my mind, tackling the toughest part of my day, my intense gym class, at the crack of dawn sets the tone for conquering anything else that comes my way. Breaking through the mental and physical barriers first thing in the morning means everything else I come across in the day feels easier.

I also draw inspiration from my relentless gym instructor, Amber, a mother of two who knows how to make you break a sweat. Her words echo in my head: 'Exercise early in the morning before your brain figures out what you're doing!' And during the class, she pushes us past our mental barriers with reminders like, 'You're up early to be here, so make it count!', driving us further than we thought possible.

Then there's Larraine, a radiant 74 year old who never misses a class. Her unwavering presence and commitment to continual self-improvement is inspiring. Given her retired status, she has the flexibility to hit the gym at any time of the day, yet she chooses the 6 am classes to stick to the routine she's always known, because she knows it sets her up for a positive day. Her dedication is a daily reminder that consistency breeds success, regardless of age or circumstance.

Humans are not designed to remain stationary and still for extended periods! Movement is inherent to our evolution and survival. Movement, in all its forms, is vital for your physical and emotional wellbeing. Whether it's the rhythm of dance, the exhilaration of cycling or the camaraderie of sports, identify and commit to a regular form of exercise at a time that suits your schedule. (If you haven't exercised for a while or are managing various health conditions, make sure you consult with your GP and take their advice on the level of exercise you should start off with.)

Even if you're pressed for time, and once you have the all-clear from your GP, try to carve out a 20-minute window each day for physical activity that gets your heart pumping. This could be squeezed in between work commitments, before or after study sessions or during breaks throughout your day. Once you've identified a suitable slot, prioritise your activities around it, remembering regular movement is vital for your body's wellbeing.

Consider simple and easy adjustments to your daily routine to incorporate more physical activity. For instance, after a focused work or study session, try doing ten star jumps, or the dreaded burpees to invigorate your body. Opt for jogging or walking instead of driving for errands whenever possible. Take the stairs instead of the escalator or elevator and park further away from your destination or jump off public transport a stop or two earlier to sneak in extra steps.

Additionally, integrate movement as much as possible into your work environment—for example, by standing up and stretching every hour, holding walking meetings instead of gathering in a conference room, or using a standing desk to alternate between sitting and standing. You can even infuse movement into household tasks such as by dancing while cooking, or using a fitness stability ball instead of a chair to work or the sofa when watching TV, to strengthen your core.

Reflect on your daily routine and consider what small adjustments you can make to increase your opportunities for regular physical activity. What changes come to mind? And what could you implement today?

## The power of feeding

What you feed your body and mind is crucial to your productivity and overall wellbeing. A balanced diet ensures your body receives the nutrition it needs to function at its best.

Appropriate nutrition also supports your brain's health and improves cognitive function. Nutrients such as omega-3 fatty acids, antioxidants, and vitamins and minerals improve memory formation and recall, focus, and overall mental sharpness and clarity, all vital for optimal productivity. Certain nutrients, such as complex carbohydrates and amino acids, can influence the neurotransmitter levels in your brain, affecting your mood and emotional wellbeing. Eating well—enjoying food that nourishes you, and is high in protein, minerals and vitamins yet low in refined sugar and fatty acids—is key to a well-balanced diet. Eating a balanced diet can help you stabilise your mood and reduce the risk of mood disorders such as depression and anxiety, which in turn inevitably impact productivity.

By fuelling your body with the right nutrients, you can optimise your physical and mental health, enabling you to perform at your best in all aspects of life.

Eating a well-balanced diet is not always easy, but here are some tips to help:

- *Plan ahead and batch cook:* Planning and preparing your meals in advance can help you maintain consistency in your eating habits. Cooking a few dish servings in one go can also save you time throughout the week. You can use the leftovers for future meals or freeze them for later use. This eliminates the need to start from scratch every day and allows you to reheat and eat when you're short on time.

- *Have a shopping list:* When you plan your meals, create a shopping list based on the ingredients you'll use so you have this list on hand next time you're at the supermarket or ordering online. This will save you time and help you avoid buying items on a whim that go unused and get thrown away.

Planning your meals ahead of time can help alleviate the stress and uncertainty that often accompanies mealtime decisions. This practice is especially beneficial during busy periods—which for you may feel like an almost constant state of being. When overwhelmed by other responsibilities and deadlines, the last thing you want to worry about is what you and your loved ones will eat. In such moments, opting for the most convenient and easy option often becomes the default choice. However, these options may not always be the healthiest unless planned and prepared in advance. Remember, the key lies in the art of planning and, whenever possible, meal preparation.

Although not suitable for all people, intermittent fasting can provide some benefits. This approach, such as the 16:8 pattern, cycles between periods of eating and fasting.

Reported benefits of intermittent fasting include improved mental clarity and focus, with fasting helping to increase alertness and reduce brain fog by triggering the release of certain neurotransmitters and hormones, such as norepinephrine and cortisol. Studies have shown fasting can also help regulate blood sugar levels and insulin sensitivity, leading to more stable energy levels throughout the day. This stability helps prevent energy crashes and fluctuations associated with eating multiple meals, allowing for sustained alertness and productivity.

In addition, fasting can simplify your daily routine by reducing the number of meals you need to plan and prepare. With fewer meals to consider, you may find yourself with more time and mental energy to focus on other tasks. This can enhance productivity and enable you to accomplish everything you set out to do for the day, especially when you eat healthy, well-balanced and nutritious meals.

If considering adopting an intermittent fasting approach, first check with your GP or other healthcare professionals such as a nutritionist or dietitian. These experts are best placed to advise on the right diet for you, based on your existing lifestyle and health, and can guide you as you make changes. Consulting with a health practitioner can also help you identify specific changes that could uplift and enhance your current diet. Remember—seeking professional advice is crucial for making informed decisions about your nutrition and overall wellbeing.

What does your current diet consist of, and do you think it could be enhanced in a small way?

## The power of cultivating internal calm: BPM

I believe there are three secret weapons for staying cool, calm and collected in a chaotic world where you are constantly being pulled in many different directions. Collectively, I call these secret weapons 'BPM'—standing for **b**reath, being **p**resent, and **m**editation.

Each of these three secret weapons is a superpower everyone possesses within them, including you. You can apply any one of these for as little as two to three minutes at a time, several times a day, or as and when you need them. Using them allows you to swiftly hack your body and brain connection and bring calm, focus and balance, providing instant relief. Empower yourself by cultivating these three secret weapons as part of your toolkit to thrive in any situation.

### Breath

Picture this: you carve out a little slice of quiet time for yourself, close your eyes and breathe. With each inhale and exhale, you feel more present and grounded. It is like giving your brain a little vacation from all the chaos. Ensure your exhaled breath is a few seconds longer than your inhaled breath to activate your parasympathetic nervous system and enjoy the real benefit of deep and calming breathing.

### Present

Being present is about being aware of what's happening right now without getting caught up in the past or worrying about the future. So, take a moment to really savour the sights, sounds and sensations around you, soaking them all in like a sponge.

### Meditation

Close your eyes and bring your attention and focus to the eye centre—the space behind your forehead and in the middle of your eyebrows. Focusing on this space enables you to be centred. Take a deep breath and exhale. Let yourself know you are capable, you have strength, you have courage, you will thrive, and life is full of Yin and Yang. Brighter moments and brighter days are just around the corner. By tuning your attention inwards to your eye centre, you can tap into a deep sense of calm and clarity, no matter what's happening around you.

## The power of quality connection and community

We live in a world where communication is at our fingertips, screens bridge distances, we are surrounded by diverse communities and our lives are more interconnected than ever before. However, we are also witnessing an astonishing rise in human loneliness. Studies show that 33 per cent of the world's population experiences loneliness every day. Social isolation and loneliness can make dealing with tough situations more challenging by reducing your ability to adapt effectively.

Your fundamental need for belonging and feeling that you matter remains unchanged from your childhood days on the playground. As adults, we spend most of our waking hours in the workplace or places of study seeking connections, friendships, recognition, validation and a sense of being valued and having purpose. Our quest for belonging, connection and a sense of community drives us to seek out meaningful interactions with others.

Research consistently emphasises the significant link between social interactions and overall health and wellbeing. A particularly striking finding comes from a comprehensive meta-analysis, which examined

148 studies involving over 300 000 participants. Surprisingly, it revealed that the quality of a person's social relationships is a more accurate predictor of mortality than factors such as smoking, alcohol consumption or high blood pressure. Loneliness is ranked similarly to other risk factors such as physical inactivity or obesity. (For more detail from this meta-analysis, see 'Social relationships and mortality risk: a meta-analytic review', by Julianne Holt-Lunstad, Timothy Smith and J Bradley Layton.)

Having multiple positive social interactions every day boosts your happiness and feeling of belonging. It's not just about how many interactions you have, however, but also how positive they are. Each positive interaction has the potential to reinforce you belong. When you feel connected and included, you feel better about yourself and more capable of reaching your goals.

Even though many people think they are inclusive of most people (even those quite different to them), research shows we often miss the mark. We tend to believe we're less biased than we actually are, and we're more likely to associate and connect with people who are like us. This leads to what I call 'hollow inclusion'. It means your unconscious biases influence your interactions, so you only scratch the surface in your relationships instead of really getting to know others deeply, especially those different to you. This shallow level of engagement can leave you and others feeling empty, lonely and a longing to truly belong. Recognising and addressing your biases (conscious and unconscious) can lead to deeper, more meaningful connections with others, fostering a sense of belonging and fulfilment for all not just those most similar to yourself.

The profound impact of connection and community was beautifully embodied by my beloved grandma, Mama, who is no longer on this earth. Born in India, she moved continents in pursuit of a better life for her family, migrating to East Africa before eventually settling in the United Kingdom with her five sons. Though I never had the privilege of meeting my grandfather, who worked as an engineer for East African Airlines in the 1960s, his enduring support from afar enabled our Mama to provide for her family.

Mama was a remarkable woman, radiating gentleness yet brimming with inner strength and courage. She nurtured her five sons into kind-hearted men, one of whom is my wonderful father. Mama's love extended to all her grandchildren and great-grandchildren. I often recall her gathering us, creating a fist with one hand and clasping her other hand around it while uttering the words 'ik mutt'—the literal translation of which is 'one fist'—to symbolise 'togetherness'. Mama's philosophy united our family, fostering unity, strength and support for each other, even today as our extended family members live across several continents.

The ethos of 'ik mutt' holds a special place in the hearts of all of us grandchildren, serving as a cherished legacy that we aspire to pass down to future generations. Together, we understand that unity fosters resilience and enhances our ability to accomplish our goals while uplifting and supporting each other.

Take a moment to reflect on the strength of your own connections and community. Can you invest time and energy into cultivating a more robust support network around you? Can you infuse the spirit of 'ik mutt' into your treasured relationships, nurturing greater solidarity and collective support with the common goal of lifting each other?

At the heart of meaningful relationships and a strong community lies reciprocity—a principle where each person both gives and receives support, care and attention. Reciprocal relationships, built on mutual respect, stand the test of time. When you feel valued and appreciated through this mutual exchange, you're more likely to invest in nurturing and maintaining these relationships for the long term. This sense of togetherness ensures you're supported by others who champion your dreams and offer resources to help you succeed, just as you do for them. Such relationships are invaluable and priceless; count yourself truly blessed to have them in your life.

On a lighter note, did you know that children laugh 300 times a day, while, as adults, we barely manage 17 chuckles? It's so important to change this because laughter is not just joy; it's a power station for your mind and body. When you laugh, serotonin and endorphins are released, boosting your mood, creativity and positivity. So try to giggle more and find humour in the everyday mundane—you'll invite more joy into your life, one chuckle at a time.

## *The power of learning*

Remaining open to new insights, perspectives, skills and experiences is crucial for your personal growth, productivity and overall sense of joy. Continuously seeking to acquire and apply your knowledge keeps your mind sharp and agile. Every new insight, interaction or experience sparks neural activity, forming new connections and pathways in your brain. Embracing a lifelong learning mindset is essential for staying open-minded, curious and adaptable.

When you adopt this approach to learning, you'll discover countless possibilities for tackling challenges that come your way. Surround yourself with individuals more knowledgeable than yourself to foster growth and share your knowledge through mentoring others.

◆ ◆ ◆

The power of the oxygen mask resides within each of us, irrespective of social class, status, gender, age or background.

What steps can you take to ensure that you upgrade and maintain your oxygen mask? These steps will help you achieve more of what matters to you and brings you joy.

# CHAPTER 9

# End the day on reflection

Can you think of a time when you looked back and thought, *If only I had said that (or not), acted in this way or knew what I know now*? Would you have handled things differently or made different choices? As I often remind my clients, 'True learning unfolds in the moments of reflection, not in the heat of the actual moment'.

As an example of this, Farhana recalls a situation where she disagreed with a friend who had expressed some judgements on her planning and organisation of an upcoming event. In the heat of the argument, Farhana responded impulsively, saying hurtful things without considering the consequences. Later, on reflection, she realised that if she had taken a moment to pause and respond more calmly or empathetically, the situation might not have unfolded as it did, possibly leading to a more constructive conversation and preserving their friendship.

Or take Jason, who went for a job interview. He felt nervous and stumbled over his responses, failing to convey his skills and experiences effectively. On reflection, he realised that if he had prepared more thoroughly or practised his answers beforehand, he would have presented himself more confidently and compellingly.

Reflection is a powerful tool for learning and growth. When you take the time to pause and contemplate your day and your experiences, you allow yourself the opportunity to extract meanings, insights and lessons that might have been overlooked during the moment itself.

During these moments of reflection, you gain a deeper understanding, make connections and identify areas for improvement. You enhance your learning and self-awareness, which enables you to navigate future challenges with greater wisdom and resilience. Reflection often leads to the benefit of hindsight. Through the process, you uncover insights and perspectives that were not apparent to you in that moment. You can recognise that you could have done something differently and learn how you might approach similar situations in the future.

In this way, reflection is intentional introspection, an inward practice for exploring your thoughts, emotions and experiences. Research has shown that reflection also helps regulate your emotions and accelerate cognitive development.

In this chapter, I outline my Trio Reflection Technique to help you intentionally close your day. While the 5Qs Formula primes you to be the best version of you at the start of the day, the Trio Reflection Technique can help lift your mood and focus your attention positively at the end of each day. It gives you the gift of understanding yourself that little bit more. After applying this technique, you are likely to experience better-quality sleep, develop an optimistic mindset and wake up feeling more resilient.

# Trio Reflection Technique

The Trio Reflection Technique (TRT) only takes five to ten minutes to complete each evening. It involves asking yourself three simple questions as you pause to reflect on your day.

The three questions that make up my TRT are as follows:

1. What one thing went well today?

2. What could have gone better?

3. What did you learn about yourself?

Question one helps you focus on the day's positives and reflect on something meaningful and important to you that went well.

Question two helps you recognise opportunities to do something better or differently. This also addresses the principle that you are continually on a learning growth journey.

Question three helps you develop self-awareness. It prompts you to observe changes in your responses to situations or shifts in your priorities. This question acknowledges the continual evolution of your identity, keeping you attuned to yourself, especially as you face different phases in your life.

The science behind each of these questions is similar to that already shared for the 5Qs Formula, specifically in relation to questions three and five (refer to chapters 5 and 7). One important further aspect to consider is that of finding distance from your day as you reflect on it.

In *The Practice of Adaptive Leadership*, Alexander Grashow, Ronald Heifetz and Marty Linsky coined the phrase 'Moving from the dance floor to the balcony' as part of the development of adaptive leadership theory, based on their research conducted at Harvard University. Often, daily life can feel like you're in the middle of a crowded dance floor, being pulled in all different directions, and tending to only see and pay attention to what is in close proximity to you.

When you're on the dance floor, it's easy to get caught up in the here and now, losing sight of the bigger picture. Moving away from the dance floor and up on to the metaphorical balcony every evening allows you to look at situations or experiences more objectively and holistically. Seeing them from a balcony view allows you to view things from a broader, wider lens, whereby you are more likely to spot trends and patterns, which can help shape your thinking and inform your decision-making. Being on the balcony helps you create some distance from your day, and so view it as an observer, not as the person experiencing it. It's akin to being a camera operator, watching and observing your day from an external perspective.

This aspect of distance can help detach you from the emotions and feelings that may otherwise influence your judgements and cloud your thinking. You're likely to perceive things from a more balanced and rational perspective through this lens. While time can naturally heal upsetting or unsettling situations, the most significant healing often comes from your ability to shift your perspectives and consider the same situation from different interpretations, including those of others, or alternative variables.

When you look at different perspectives from the balcony view, things start to become clearer and make more sense to you.

When reading Stephen Covey's *The 7 Habits of Highly Effective People* at the age of 16, I first encountered the concept of perspective changes, or as Covey calls them 'paradigm shifts'. As I mentioned way back in the preface, the teachings in Covey's book profoundly shaped my personal growth and development from adolescence to adulthood. Offering countless invaluable insights, I highly recommend reading the book for yourself, if you haven't already.

One particular story from the book resonated deeply with me— Covey's account of a father and his two children he saw on a New York subway. Covey describes the children as being loud and rambunctious. They were yelling at each other, and even grabbing people's papers as they sat near him on the subway. The father sat beside Covey with closed eyes and did nothing to control his children. Covey shares that he found it difficult not to feel irritated and to think, *Why is this father not taking any responsibility for his children?* So finally, Covey said, 'Sir, your children are really disturbing a lot of people. I wonder if you couldn't control them a little more?'

The father lifted his gaze as if to become conscious of the situation for the first time and said softly, 'Oh, you're right. I guess I should do something about it. We just came from the hospital where their mother died about an hour ago. I don't know what to think, and I guess they don't know how to handle it either.' At that very moment, Covey shares how he suddenly saw things differently: he thought differently, felt differently and behaved differently. His irritation had vanished, and his heart was filled with the man's pain. Everything for him changed in that very moment, when he realised what the father and the children were going through.

Reflecting back, it was this story that ignited my passion for understanding human psychology and personal growth. Covey's anecdote about the grieving father and his children on a New York subway significantly impacted me; his shift in perspective from irritation to compassionate understanding clearly highlighted the transformative power of empathy.

It was then I became deeply interested in understanding the complexities of empathy—the ability to see the world, as well as specific moments, through the eyes of others without losing yourself in emotion. I realised that empathy isn't just about understanding; it's also about empowering yourself and others by truly listening and offering genuine compassion and understanding. A clear distinction exists between offering someone sympathy and empathy. The former often leads to feelings of pity and emotional overwhelm, which actually unintentionally disempowers the person you are sympathetic too. However, when you empathise with others, they feel empowered, supported and heard, which leaves them feeling empowered. I learnt to appreciate the power of empathy, an essential life skill that would enable me to better connect with others and make a positive impact on myself and those around me.

Encouraging yourself to step up on to the metaphorical balcony each evening is a powerful way to empower yourself. By embracing different paradigm shifts, you'll attain a clearer, more rational and balanced perspective of your day. This approach enables you to discover ways to enhance your productivity and experience more joy and fulfilment each day.

Meet my client Tristan, who knows all too well the pressures of a demanding career and a hectic lifestyle. As a high-powered executive at a bustling tech firm, her days are filled with back-to-back meetings, urgent emails and tight deadlines. Despite her professional success, Tristan often feels overwhelmed and disconnected from herself.

One evening, feeling the world's weight on her shoulders, Tristan decides to try something different. She sets aside five minutes for the TRT exercise, guided by its three simple questions:

1. What one thing went well today?

2. What could have gone better?

3. What did you learn about yourself?

As Tristan delves into her reflections, she uncovers moments of triumph and challenge. She recalls the satisfaction of successfully presenting her team's project proposal, yet recognises the need to temper her perfection during a particularly stressful meeting. Most importantly, she learns that she tends to be overly critical of herself, a realisation that opens the door to greater self-compassion and acceptance.

Over time, Tristan integrates the TRT questions into her daily evening routine. She finds solace in the quiet moments of introspection, gaining clarity and perspective among the chaos of her busy life. With each reflection, she grows more resilient and self-aware, navigating her challenges with grace and courage. As Tristan's journey unfolds, she discovers that reflection is not just a one-time exercise but has the potential to be a practice in her life.

Reflection is a practice that invites you to embrace your humanity, with all its joys and struggles, to develop a deeper understanding of yourself and the world around you. Through reflection, you awaken the beauty of your own existence, finding meaning and purpose in the tapestry of everyday life.

You will find sanctuary in the stillness of reflection each evening. In the quiet depths of your soul, you can discover a deeper understanding of yourself and the boundless potential within. I encourage you to try the practice of reflection with the effective TRT tool, with an open heart and curious mind, knowing that together with the 5Qs Formula, it has the potential to transform not only your life but also the world around you.

# Conclusion

The 5Qs Formula provides you with the tools to optimise and prime how you feel, think and act, mobilising you to seize each day as a chance to refine your mindset, actions and presence. With this formula, you gain control and agency over your life, especially your productivity and a sense of daily joy. Enabling you to do more of what matters and brings you joy.

Time and time again, I've witnessed how the 5Qs Formula has transformed people's lives. Whether you're a busy professional, leader, parent, business owner or student juggling life's demands and feeling stuck in survival mode, the 5Qs Formula has the power to make a profound difference to what you can achieve, helping you to be 5 per cent more awesome each day!

Specifically, the 5Qs Formula helps you reclaim your time by prioritising what truly matters to you and your goals. It also helps strengthen your relationships with others by reducing friction, enabling you to be fully present, engaged, and your best self. Personally, I've experienced my relationship with my husband grow to deeper levels of understanding, compassion, love and partnership.

Leaders who implement the 5Qs Formula have become better at emotional regulation, navigating stress and pressure, while also enhancing their ability to bring out the best in those around them. Parents have become calmer, more present and balanced, experiencing improved communication, understanding and mutual respect with their children. Busy business owners have become better at managing their stress levels, avoiding burnout and instead feeling more energised and accomplished, both at work and home. Students have become better at being productive, making the most of the time they have to be focused and impactful while still being able to enjoy the phase of life they find themselves in.

For all these reasons, I'm so excited for you to experience even just some of these results. My aim was to make the formula as accessible, practical and implementable as possible, and this is why I'm proud to say it will only take you five minutes a day to apply it and experience all its benefits. Amidst your busy life, I know you can spare five minutes to invest in yourself at the start of your day, to apply the 5Qs Formula, especially now you know all the benefits it will bring to you and those around you.

Now that you've read the book and hopefully completed the self-reflection exercises, nothing stands in your way to moving from surviving to thriving, overwhelm to feeling in control, scattered to intentional and reactive to responsive. You can now recognise and acknowledge your current emotions, set goals based on your values and prioritise in a way that honours your time.

My aim has been for *Productivity Joy* to take you on the journey to overcome procrastination and stay focused, improve mood, increase your effectiveness and to be purposeful, to enable you to show up as the best version of yourself and craft your day for maximum impact. The 5Qs Formula is the key to unlocking your full productivity power, priming you to feel accomplished, energised and intentional each day.

You can start putting the 5Qs Formula into play right now. I hope you've been inspired by all the research, practical tips, insights and stories—my own and those of some of my clients. Like you, we are ordinary people now able to do extraordinary things for ourselves and others. I always say, if I can transform, you can too. Gift yourself the experience of being effective and feeling energised each and every day—as my clients tell me, the 5Qs Formula is a 'game-changer', making you primed, intentional and energised for productivity and joy! They say it helps them not only be 1 per cent better each day, but each question accumulates to a 5 per cent increase in daily productivity and joy.

I've also seen people quickly reboot their energy and focus with an immediate positive impact, especially after a tough day or a rough morning, by applying the 5Qs Formula. So, don't worry if you forget to use it some days; you can easily pick it up again at any time. Just don't let it go completely, because you'll be doing a disservice to yourself and those around you.

In addition to completing the 5Qs Formula, maintain your oxygen mask and practise the end of day Trio Reflection Technique to take care of your holistic wellbeing. When your wellbeing is strong, productivity, performance and satisfaction is high—and you are able to bring your A game, every day.

It deeply concerns me that 82 per cent of professionals (according to the 2024 Global Talent Trends report published by Mercer) feel stressed, overwhelmed and risk of burnout (just like I did, before I developed the 5Qs Formula). As I mentioned at the start of this book, this results in a lack of productivity, and an increase in procrastination, costing Australian businesses approximately $60 billion dollars annually and costing US employers around USD $1.8 trillion annually. But more than this, it robs us all of our daily joy!

As you've read this book now, you will also know that productivity is not about doing more hard work and getting through a never ending to do list and feeling exhausted and unsatisfied. It's essentially about doing more of what matters to you and magnifies your joy!

My mission is to help five million busy professionals benefit from the 5Qs Formula.

You can support me in my mission by sharing this book and its insights with others by posting a photograph of Productivity Joy on your socials and tagging myself too.

I firmly believe in the ripple effect of positive change. So, I'd like to encourage you to share your learnings, insights and reflections from this book with others in your personal and professional life. In this way, you help yourself and those around you live a more enriched, intentional, productive and joyful life each day and together we lift humanity.

I've also included helpful resources you can access from simirayat .com or scan the QR code below.

Please do stay in touch with me and reach out if I can provide further support or help you bring greater joy to your workplace. There is no reason to feel you are on this journey alone.

I'm looking forward to staying in touch and cheering you on from the sidelines as you, too, transform your impact, productivity and joy to be 5 per cent more awesome each day!

With much gratitude and appreciation.

Simi Rayat
simirayat.com
simi@simirayat.com

# Appendix: Typical values

The following table provides a list of typical values I have identified and my description for each. To help determine your values, you can add your rating to each one: using 'D' for deal-breaker, 'S' for so/so and 'N' for nah.

**Typical values and their descriptions**

| Value and description | Rating: D, S or N |
|---|---|
| Accepting: to accept myself and be accepting of others, without judgement | |
| Admire: to actively seek out the beauty and positivity in myself, others and in my environment | |
| Adventurous: to actively seek out new experiences that bring excitement as well as fear! | |
| Agile: to be flexible to adapt and be responsive to changing circumstances | |
| Be curious: to be open-minded, inquisitive and ready to discover | |
| Be real: to be authentic and genuine to who I am | |
| Collaborate: to be keen to work well with others | |
| Compassionate: to show kindness, empathy and understanding to myself and others | |

| Value and description | Rating: D, S or N |
|---|---|
| Conforming: to diligently follow the rules | |
| Contribute: to give assistance where possible to make a positive difference | |
| Courage: to tap into my inner strength, even when it scares me to do so | |
| Creative: to think outside of the box, looking to do or create something different | |
| Encouraging: to reinforce and reward progress, effort and attitude | |
| Equality: to seek to achieve sameness for everyone | |
| Equity: to treat myself and others fairly | |
| Excitement: to anticipate fun, joy, happiness or thrills | |
| Forgiving: to make peace with myself and others and move forward | |
| Freedom: to choose for myself | |
| Friendly: to be pleasant, positive and engaging with others (to get others onside) | |
| Fun: to not take life seriously, seeking ways for more laughter and play, which makes my heart smile | |
| Generous: to give with one hand without my other hand realising it | |
| Gratitude: to express appreciation for all the things I appreciate in my life, and in others | |
| Hard-working: to work hard, put in maximum effort and aim for quality outputs | |
| Honesty: to be truthful in my thoughts and actions | |
| Humbleness: to stay grounded, thankful and grateful | |
| Humorous: to appreciate the fun things in life and situations | |
| Independent: to be confident in my own decisions and doing things for myself | |
| Intimacy: to connect with others deeply, emotionally and or physically | |
| Justice: to stand by what is fair and just | |
| Kindness: to be caring to myself, others and the environment | |
| Love: to lead from the heart and act out of affection for myself or others | |
| Mindfulness: to be connected to the present | |
| Open-minded: to be willing to consider alternative perspectives | |
| Order: to be organised and planned | |
| Patient: to wait calmly for what I want or need | |

| Value and description | Rating: D, S or N |
|---|---|
| Peace: to aim for harmony, with little or no friction with myself and others | |
| Persistence: to keep trying and not give up | |
| Personal growth: to actively seek opportunities and experiences to grow, learn and elevate myself | |
| Playing big: to be bold in my thinking and actions to achieve my goals | |
| Pleasure: to seek and give enjoyment to myself or others | |
| Power: to have control, and to exert authority and influence | |
| Present: to be fully engaged with whatever I am doing and who I am with | |
| Push boundaries: to continuously question and challenge myself to grow | |
| Reciprocity: to show mutual balance of respect and regard in relationships | |
| Respect: to be considerate and show positive regard to self and others | |
| Responsible: to take ownership and accountability over responsibilities | |
| Romantic: to be open to display and express affection to others | |
| Safety: to feel secure, protected and supported | |
| Self-aware: to be in tune with how I am feeling, thinking and acting, and what I am projecting to others | |
| Self-agency: to act and focus on what is in my control | |
| Sensual: to seek ways to stimulate my five senses and stay in tune to them | |
| Sexual: to be open to exploring or expressing my sexuality | |
| Simplicity: to make the complex simple, applicable and doable | |
| Skilful: to use all personal resources to be helpful to myself and others | |
| Spiritual: to connect with the universe or something bigger than myself | |
| Stamina: to look after my physical fitness | |
| Straightforward: to clearly communicate what I want or need to others | |
| Supportive: to be encouraging and helpful to myself and others | |
| Trust: to be consistently truthful, reliable and loyal | |
| Wellbeing: to prioritise my self-care and wellbeing | |

# Further reading

Arbinger Institute, arbinger.com.

Clear, James (2018), *Atomic Habits: An Easy and Proven Way to Build Good Habits and Break Bad Ones*, Random House UK.

Covey, Stephen (2020), *The 7 Habits of Highly Effective People*, 30th anniversary edition, Simon & Schuster Australia.

Csikszentmihalyi, Mihaly (2008), *Flow: The Psychology of Optimal Experience*, Harper Perennial Modern Classics.

Dweck, Carol (2017), *Mindset: Changing the Way You Think to Fulfil Your Potential*, Little Brown.

Fiske, Susan and Taylor, Shelley (2020), *Social Cognition: From Brains to Culture*, Sage.

Flett, Gordon (2022), 'An introduction, review, and conceptual analysis of mattering as an essential construct and an essential way of life', *Journal of Psychoeducational Assessment*, 40(1), 3–36.

Fox, Glenn, Kaplan, Jonas, Damasio, Hanna and Damasio, Antonio (2015), 'Neural correlates of gratitude', *Front Psychol*, Sep 30;6:1491.

Harris, Russ (2010), *The Confidence Gap: From Fear to Freedom*, Penguin Australia.

Hawkins, David (2024), *The Highest Level of Enlightenment: Transcend the Levels of Consciousness for Total Self-Realization*, Hay House LLC.

Heifetz, Ronald, Linsky, Marty and Grashow, Alexander (2009), *The Practice of Adaptive Leadership: Tools and Tactics for Changing Your Organization and the World*, Harvard Business Review Press.

Huberman, Andrew (2024), *Huberman Lab Podcast*.

McKeown, Greg (2021), *Essentialism: The Disciplined Pursuit of Less*, Random House UK.

Mugumbate, Jacob and Nyanguru, Andrew (2013), 'Exploring African philosophy: The value of ubuntu in social work', *African Journal of Social Work*, 3 (1), 82–100.

Nickerson, Charlotte (2023), 'The Yerkes-Dodson law of arousal and performance', Simply Psychology, simplypsychology.org/what-is-the-yerkes-dodson-law.html.

Rayat, Simi (2022), 'Are you stuck in an "inclusion delusion"?', Forbes.

Rayat, Simi (2022), 'The powerful connection between inclusion and well-being', Forbes.

Rayat, Simi (2021), 'Are organizational leaders asking the right questions?', Forbes.

Rayat, Simi (2021), 'Stop focusing on your goals', Forbes.

Siegel, Daniel and Payne Bryson, Tina (2012), *The Whole-Brain Child: 12 Revolutionary Strategies to Nurture Your Child's Developing Mind*, Scribe Publications.

# 5Qs template

You can use the following template (overleaf) when answering the five questions from the 5Qs Formula each morning. Also keep in mind the PRIME acronym as a memory prompt any time you are away from this template or your journal, and are getting ready to prime your brain for the day ahead:

- **P:** Pinpoint emotions and feelings.

- **R:** Recognise gratitude.

- **I:** Identify what is working and could be working better.

- **M:** Make a list of three high-impact tasks for today.

- **E:** Envision how you want to show up today.

You can also scan the QR code to download a copy of this template.

# Your 5Qs for today

**Q1** What is your emotional temperature, and what are you feeling today?

---

**Q2a** What experiences, things or people in your life are you grateful for because they inspire you to be a better version of yourself ?

**Q2b** Think of a time you have received gratitude and appreciation from someone; how did it make you feel?

---

**Q3** What is working well for you right now, and what could be working better for you?

---

**Q4** What three things do you want to achieve today?

---

**Q5** How will you show up today?

---

# Your 5Qs for today

**Q1**    What is your emotional temperature, and what are you feeling today?

------------------------------------------------

------------------------------------------------

**Q2a**    What experiences, things or people in your life are you grateful for because they inspire you to be a better version of yourself ?

**Q2b**    Think of a time you have received gratitude and appreciation from someone; how did it make you feel?

------------------------------------------------

------------------------------------------------

**Q3**    What is working well for you right now, and what could be working better for you?

------------------------------------------------

------------------------------------------------

**Q4**    What three things do you want to achieve today?

------------------------------------------------

------------------------------------------------

**Q5**    How will you show up today?

------------------------------------------------

------------------------------------------------

# Work with Simi

Simi's passion is all about helping leaders to become a joy to work for and do business with. In this way, she helps to create cultures of high engagement, performance and wellbeing. She works at the organisational, team and individual level.

Simi works specifically with people leaders, business owners and those looking to be the best inclusive leaders they can become.

Simi can support you and your organisation in three ways:

1. Ignite your event, conference or offsite and invite Simi to be your inspiring and engaging keynote speaker.

2. Empower and equip your leaders and teams with 'masterful masterclasses' on topics such as:

   • productivity joy

   • inclusive cultures

   • human connection

   • wellbeing, mindset and peak performance.

3.  One-to-one personalised transformational leadership coaching for those looking to increase their leadership impact tenfold.

If you'd like to receive more tips and strategies to experience greater productivity joy, you can sign up to Simi's regular newsletter at simirayat.com and perhaps you'd like to discuss bringing more joy into your workplace too.

Stay in touch with Simi through any of the following:

- linkedin.com/in/simirayatbusinesspsychologist

- Instagram: instagram.com/simirayat_cpsychol/

- YouTube: @simi-rayat

# Index

'acknowledge it, to regulate it' 41–43

action bias 122–124, 126–127

action-orientation 126–128

'aha' moment 5–8

'all or nothing' thinking 86, 90

amygdala hijack 46

anger 31, 43

'The Annual Rayat Retreat' 131

anterior cingulate cortex 64

anxiety 52, 123

*Atomic Habits* (Clear) 12

Australian workforce 4

automated financial systems 125

balanced diet 201–202

books
- commit to growth 18
- highlight sections 18
- reading 16
- self-reflection exercises 17
- tools 18
- using journal 17

BPM. *see* Breath, present, meditation (BPM)

breathing 31

breath, present, meditation (BPM) 204–205

Brown, Brené 81, 150

Bryson, Tina Payne 41

Buehner, Carl W. 182

burnout, productivity *versus* 4–5

business' day-to-day operations 141

butterflies 30

chronic anger 31

Clear, James 12, 13

Clifton, Donald O. 177

CliftonStrengths assessment 177, 179

cognitive consistency theory 173

cognitive dissonance 173–174

cognitive errors 85

cognitive reframing 89

compartmentalisation

— benefits of 108

— and integration 108

— short-term 104–109

— skills during pandemic
105

constructive feedback 110

counteracting negative
thoughts 179–180

Covey, Stephen 212

Csikszentmihalyi, Mihaly 177

curiosity 171

CWS strategy 106, 108

daily parenting approach 160

daily values alignment 163–176

Damasio, Antonio 64

decision making

— approaches 124

— leadership 167

disgust 32

disjointed planning 121

Dodson, John 44

domino effect 180–183

Dweck, Carol 109

economic climate changes 4

education/economic
differences 162

Eisenhower method 142

'emotional contagion' 36, 67

emotional intelligence 47–48,
108, 182, 187

emotional radiator 37–38

emotional regulation 38–52

— 'acknowledge it, to
regulate it' 41–43

— emotional
intelligence 47–48

— 'meaning-making
machine' 40–41

— move, breathe, visual
(MBV) expansion 51–52

— productive *versus*
unproductive
emotions 43–47

emotional self-awareness 40, 43

emotional temperature 41, 54

— check-in 47

— emotional regulation 38–52

— and feelings 23–24

— 'worry time' 54

Emotional Vibration Analysis
Frequency Scale 33

emotional wellbeing 10, 141

emotions 11

— acknowledging and
labelling 54

— experience 26

— and feelings 18, 23–26, 40

— impact productivity 26–27

—intensity of 40

—productive *versus*
unproductive 43–47

—before tasks and
activities 28–29

—'worry time' 54

empathy 48, 67, 104, 160, 161,
176, 185, 187

employee retention 168

environmental hazards 85

environmental, social and
governance (ESG) 125

'essential intent,' concept of 132

external environment 167

fail-proof formula 11

fears 32, 62, 73

feedback sessions 161

feeding power 201–204

feelings 71

—annoyance and
frustration 35

—defined as 11

—disagreement 39

—emotions and
18, 23–26, 40

—experience 7–8

—interpersonal 67

—of overwhelm and
stress 135

—recognising 8

—ring of emotions and
16, 18

Festinger, Leon 173

Fiske, Susan 182

5Qs Formula

—'aha' moment 5–8

—book and *see* book

—component of 119

—daily habit making
12–13

—daily practice of 8

—emotional temperature 41

—emotions 23–26

—feelings 23–26

—gratitude component
of 67

—'holding space' 101

—impact of 3

—'inspire you to be a better
version of yourself' 72–78

—morning routine 8–10

—productivity *versus*
burnout 4–5

—question applying
52–55, 72–80

—realistic and aligned
planning for daily
accomplishment 135–153

—space and time to
implement 75

—'success' means 10–12

—working better 114–116

—working well 111–114

fixed *versus* growth
mindset 109

'flight or fight' response
32, 43, 46
*Flow: The Psychology of
Optimal Experience*
(Csikszentmihalyi) 177

Grashow, Alexander 211
gratitude
— and appreciation 73
— defining 58–61
— lens, reframing
experiences 70–72
— mindset 62, 70
— overwhelmed with 169
— positive
reinforcement of 65
— power of 71
— science and
benefits of 63–66
'gratitude habit' 65
growth mindset 109–111

*Happiness Trap, The*
(Harris), 71
Harris, Russ, 71
Hawkins, David R., 33
healthcare professional, 104
Heifetz, Ronald, 211
heuristics, 85
high-impact daily tasks,
139–142, 153–155
— allocating time
for, 147–149

'holding space,' 101
Huberman, Andrew, 51,
66–68, 153
human brain, 40, 62
— 'all or nothing'
thinking, 86
— deceive ways, 85–88
— mind reading, 87–88
— negativity bias *see*
negativity bias
— neuroplasticity 166
— over-generalisation 88
— primary concern 85
— primary function 61
— remarkable intelligence 61
— tendency 84
hypothalamus 65

'Ik mutt' 207
impact orientation 124–127, 130
impact *versus* urgency matrix
142–145, 156
integrate movement 201
intense reactions 32
intentional positive mindset 116
intermittent fasting
approach 203
interpersonal feelings 67

journal, 16, 17

lack of clarity 121
lack of motivation 115

language 102
leadership 132
—decision-making
processes 167
—and employees 168
—transformation 35
learned helplessness 98
*Learned Optimism* (Seligman) 98
learning 109–111
—power of 208
learning agility 91, 130, 165
lifelong learning mindset 208
Linsky, Marty 211
loneliness 206
long daily to-do list 136
love 30–31
lower vibrational emotions 33

Mayo Clinic Health System 66
McKeown, Greg 132
'meaning-making
machine' 40–41, 70
medial prefrontal cortex 64
meditation 205
mental filter 86–87
mindfulness practices 19
mind reading 87–88
mindset 11, 19
—gratitude 62
—of growth and
learning 109–111
—lifelong learning 208

—personal
responsibility and 182
—problem-focused to
solution-focused 102–103
mood disorders 202
morning routine 8–10
—advantage of 19–20
motivation 44, 45, 123
motivation–reward cycle 114
move, breathe, visual (MBV)
expansion 51–52
movement power 199–201

negative feelings 93
negativity bias 61, 83
—'all or nothing'
thinking 86, 90
—constructive
reframing 89–91
—distraction of social
comparison 93–94
—mental filter 86–87
—mind reading, 87–88
—over-generalisation 88
—power of priming 94–97
—strength 84–91
neuroimaging studies 64
neuroplasticity 166
neurotransmitters 96
neurotransmitter serotonin 65
Niequist, Shauna 81
nutrients 201

optimal thinking
orientation 124
optimism 97–101
'ordinary moments' 81
over-generalisation 88
overthinking orientation
122–124, 126–127, 129–130
oxygen mask 193
—power of 194–208

'paradigm shifts' concept
of, 212–213
paradox of perfection 91–97
parasympathetic nervous
system 204
'perception is projection' 76
personal
responsibilities 148, 159
physical discomfort 115
physical environment 112
physical exercise 10
physical hazards 85
physical inactivity 206
physical movement 51
Pink, Daniel 152
Pomodoro technique 129
positive emotions 27
positive feelings 27
positive reinforcement of
gratitude 65
power
—of cultivating internal
calm 204–205

—of feeding 201–204
—of learning 208
—of movement 199–201
—of oxygen mask 194–208
—of priming 94–97
—of quality connection and
community 205–208
—of quality sleep 194–199
*Practice of Adaptive
Leadership, The* 211
practise strategic
procrastination 128
PRIME memory 13, 18–19
priming power 94–97
prioritising 145–147
problem-focused to solution-
focused mindset 102–103
problem-solving strength 177
procrastination orientation
122–124, 126–127, 129
productive *versus* unproductive
emotions 43–47
productivity
—achieving tasks 121–122
—*versus* burnout 4–5
—emotions impact 26–27
—moving to an 'impact'
orientation 124–127
—optimism and resiliency,
link between 97–101
—orientation 124–131
—paradox of perfection
91–97

—psychological
wellbeing and 108
—purpose and goals 131–135
—thinking patterns *see*
thinking patterns
—through three
principles 121–122
—Yin and Yang of
challenge 101–109
professionals and
business owners 11
psychological hazards 85
psychological wellbeing
10, 99, 108
psychologists 167
'purposeful daily living' 160

quality sleep power, 194–199

realistic and aligned
planning 135–153
—breaking down
tasks 139–142
—regularly scrutinise
your diary 152–153
recency effect 97
reciprocal relationships
207–208
Redmond, Derek 68
Redmond, Jim 68
reflection 108, 209–210
—moments 210
relaxation techniques 9–10

resiliency 97–101
reward system 129
Ring of Emotions 16, 18,
29–33, 40, 42, 43, 53
'rule of three' memory 136

sabre-toothed tigers 62
sadness 30
science-backed hacks 51–52
secret weapons 204
self-awareness 17, 23, 32, 211
—emotion 40, 43
self-care 193
self-compassion 103–104, 108
self-confidence 99
self-esteem 45
self-reflection exercises
15, 17, 18, 172
Seligman, Martin 98
*7 Habits of Highly Effective
People, The* (Covey) 212
short-term
compartmentalisation
104–109
Siegel, Daniel J 41
skin reactions 32
SMART goals 132
social bonding 67
social comparison bias 91
social comparison
distraction 93–94
social media 92, 93
societal norms/expectations 149

stereotype content model 182

strategic family planning 132

streamlining communication
    channels 151

StrengthsFinder assessment 177

stress 44, 52, 123, 135

'success' 10–12
    —setting yourself
      up for 16–19

surprise 31

'survival mode' form 74

'sweet spot' of pressure 44

switching time 93

tangible validation 63

tensions 39

thinking patterns 121
    —action bias 122–127
    —overcoming 128–131
    —overthinking 122–127
    —procrastination 122–127

Three Anchors relaxation
    technique 197–198

transformative approach 3

Trio Reflection Technique
    (TRT) 210–215, 219

TRT see Trio Reflection
    Technique (TRT)

Ubuntu principles 185

UK adult population 4

unchecked emotions 46

unproductive emotions,
    productive versus 43–47

unrealistic planning 121

unresolved anger 31

unresolved feelings 40

valuable resource 4

values
    —alignment
      importance 167–173
    —common 221–223
    —daily alignment 163–165
    —expect 165–166
    —kindness and empathy 176
    —not connecting
      with 175–176

values congruency 167

'walk and talk' meetings 155

well-balanced diet 201–202

When: The Scientific Secrets of
    Perfect Timing (Pink) 152

Whole-Brain Child, The 41

Yerkes, Robert 44

yin and yang 101–109
    problem-focused to solution-
      focused mindset 102–103